KIIIG

CORPORATE FINANCE MANUAL

MAKING CAPITAL
BUDGETING DECISIONS

MAKING CAPITAL BUDGETING DECISIONS

MAXIMIZING THE VALUE OF THE FIRM

Dr Hazel Johnson

FINANCIAL TIMES
PRENTICE HALL

PEARSON EDUCATION LIMITED

Head Office:
Edinburgh Gate
Harlow CM20 2JE
Tel: +44 (0)1279 623623
Fax: +44 (0)1279 431059

London Office:
128 Long Acre, London WC2E 9AN
Tel: +44 (0)171 447 2000
Fax: +44 (0)171 240 5771

First published in Great Britain in 1999

ISBN 0 273 63879 3

British Library Cataloguing in Publication Data
A CIP catalogue record for this book can be obtained
from the British Library.

1 3 5 7 9 10 8 6 4 2

Typeset by Northern Phototypesetting Co Ltd.
Printed and bound in Great Britain by
Redwood Books, Trowbridge, Wiltshire.

*The Publishers' policy is to use paper manufactured
from sustainable forests.*

ABOUT THE AUTHOR

Dr Hazel J. Johnson is Distinguished University Scholar at the University of Louisville and Professor of Finance (USA). Dr Johnson was formerly a member of the finance faculty of Georgetown University (Washington, DC, USA). She has authored more than 20 books in the areas of international finance and financial institutions. With publications in the USA, Europe, Latin America, and Asia, Dr Johnson's work has been translated into Japanese and Spanish. In addition, she has developed software systems for business practitioners in the areas of bank valuation, capital budgeting, cost of capital, and mergers and acquisitions. Dr Johnson has acted as a consultant to more than 50 major US financial institutions and a number of state and federal agencies.

In loving memory of Ida W. Kelly
and Lucille V. Johnson.

CONTENTS

FOREWORD

Capital budgeting decisions involve the largest tangible investments of any firm. These decisions directly impact the value of shareholder wealth and the future viability of the firm.

Making Capital Budgeting Decisions: Maximizing the Value of the Firm helps corporate managers identify relevant cash flows and measure the value of prospective capital investments. This book provides a comprehensive array of analytical tools for project evaluation payback period (a period of time), internal rate of return (a percentage), net present value (a dollar amount), and profitability index (a ratio). The techniques are compared both pros and cons. Numerous illustrations help managers construct direct applications of the tools.

The accompanying *Capital Budgeting Software System* helps managers make the transition from concept to practice fast and easy. The Excel 7.0 based system provides a framework in which to analyze capital asset investment decisions for a project with an anticipated life of up to 40 years. Schedules detail the initial investment, any existing property that will be sold in a replacement decision, required net working capital changes, operational cash flows, and depreciation tax benefits. Cash flows are automatically analyzed and the results include internal rate of return, net present value, and profitability index.

Making Capital Budgeting Decisions: Maximizing the Value of the Firm answers three critical questions:

- How do capital budgeting decisions help managers maximize the value of the firm?
- How can the firm avoid paying too much for capital projects?
- How can the firm implement the capital budgeting concepts in the book easily?

The book and the software are engineered to provide in-depth and user-friendly support in one of the most critical areas of management decision making.

CHAPTER 1

WHY CAPITAL BUDGETING DECISIONS ARE IMPORTANT

Introduction

■

The Firm's Financial Statements

■

Maximizing Shareholder Wealth

■

The Determinants of Firm Value

■

Earnings, Stock Price, and Capital Budgeting Decisions

INTRODUCTION

Capital budgeting decisions involve some of the most significant financial decisions of a firm. Through capital budgeting decisions, a firm increases its investment in plant, property, and equipment. The global nature and the magnitude of these decisions perhaps can be best appreciated by referring to a sample announced in mid-1998.

■ ■ ■

The *UK* independent oil and gas explorer, Hardy Oil and Gas PLC, announced a decision to invest *£95 million* (approximately *$152 million*) by the end of 1998 in oil exploration and oil field appraisal and development. By the end of 2002, the total of such investments was expected to reach *£300 million* (*$480 million*). These investments were projected to support a potential five-fold increase in production by 2002.

■ ■ ■

In *South Africa*, it was announced that Vodacom, one of the country's two mobile telephone networks, had entered a contract to purchase *$75 million* of base-station equipment as part of a *$489 million* capital expenditure to expand capacity and remain competitive with its rival, Mobile Telephone Networks.

■ ■ ■

In the *USA*, Sprint Corporation – the telecommunications firm – announced that its new integrated, on-demand network would empower users simultaneously to conduct several phone calls, receive faxes, and use the Internet. The firm was pleased also to announce that the project would cost less than *$400 million* over a two-year period.

■ ■ ■

The front-runners in the bid for the right to pursue a softwood-pulp mill in *Latvia* appeared to be two foreign companies – Sodra (Sweden) and Metsae-Serla Oy (Finland). According to the tentative plans, the mill would be a joint venture among Sodra, Metsae-Serla, and the Latvian government, would be one of the world's lowest-cost producers, and was projected to require a *$1 billion* investment.

■ ■ ■

These examples illustrate the huge sums that can be involved in capital budgeting decisions. They also indicate the strategic nature of the investments. The UK oil company seeks to increase revenues. The South African telecommunications firm wants to maintain market share in an environment of expanding demand. The US firm wants to stay on the cutting edge of innovation in the highly competitive long-distance market. The Swedish and Finnish firms envision low-cost production capabilities.

Such strategies are among the most important decisions made within the firm because they have the greatest impact on the firm in the long term. Capital budgeting addresses specific decisions made within the firm in its operational arenas – from the mega-million-dollar deals noted above to decisions concerning buildings and plant to perhaps smaller decisions concerning office furnishings and equipment. The common theme in all capital budgeting decisions is the long-term commitment of corporate capital. While it is tempting to assemble a group of ideas and theories that can be applied in a scientific approach, it is vital to understand how capital budgeting decisions affect overall profitability of the firm and, ultimately, shareholder wealth.

To draw the connection between capital budgeting decisions and shareholder value, it is necessary to examine the fundamentals of the financial operations of the firm. This process begins with an examination of the firm's balance sheet and income statement.

THE FIRM'S FINANCIAL STATEMENTS

The Balance Sheet

Figure 1.1 is an example of a balance sheet. Horizon Technology is a diversified manufacturer of electronic components. Its balance sheet reflects the customary accounts that can be found in the general ledger of any non-financial corporation.

FIGURE 1.1

Horizon Technology Co. Consolidated Balance Sheet* 1998

Assets		Liabilities	
Cash	$ 50	Accounts payable	$ 10
		Accrued expenses	5
Accounts receivable	125	Notes payable	65
		Long-term debt	150
Inventory	75	*Total liabilities*	230
Fixed assets:		**Equity**	
Land	$100		
Buildings	130	Preferred stock	50
Equipment	200	Common stock	85
	430	Retained earnings	150
Acc. depreciation	(165)	*Total equity*	285
Net fixed assets	265		
		Total liabilities	
Total assets	$515	*and equity*	$515

* In millions of dollars.

Assets

The assets of the firm are resources that have been put in place to generate an earnings stream for the firm. The liabilities and equity section are sources of the financial resources that the firm has deployed.

Cash

Cash of $50 million is listed first on the balance sheet because it is the most liquid.[1] This account includes cash on hand (petty cash) and cash in bank. Since all assets are listed in order of liquidity, cash receives the first position.

Accounts Receivable

Accounts receivable of $125 million follow as the next most liquid because of the short-term nature of the asset. Most customer accounts will be collected in the normal course of business within a 90–120-day period. Accounts receivable represent the delayed cash receipts from sales of the firm. Accounts receivable are an investment in deferred cash receipts – in most cases, associated with a carrying cost to the firm. In some cases, a firm operates a financing operation that is significant in scope and earns significant interest income – but this generally is not the case. Notable exceptions include firms such as General Motors Acceptance Corporation (GMAC), the financial services arm of General Motors. The extensive activities of GMAC cause it to more closely resemble a bank than a manufacturing company. Typically, manufacturing companies do not have significant financing activities.

Inventory

Inventory is the next account, with a balance of $75 million in the case of Horizon. Inventory is also an investment that will not generate profit for the company until sold. Inventory is thus a commitment of the company to assets that presumably will be sold in the near future. Notice that inventory is listed after accounts receivable, indicating that inventory is less liquid. While accounts receivable will generally be collected at or near face value, the proceeds of inventory sales are less predictable in timing and/or amount.

---

[1] An asset is liquid to the extent that it may be easily converted into cash without loss of value.

Both accounts receivable and inventory are short-term investments that will be converted into cash in a brief period of time. Together, the three assets – cash, accounts receivable, and inventory – are often referred to as the *working capital* of the firm.

Fixed Assets

On the other hand, *fixed assets* have a much longer life and will generate cash flows for the firm for a much longer period of time. The decisions that are necessary to arrive at the correct mix of fixed assets are considerably more involved. However, examination of the balance sheet for Horizon Technology in Figure 1.1 reveals that fixed assets are the largest investment of the firm. The fixed asset investments for most manufacturing firms represent the heart of operating activities and generate revenues through production of a particular product line (inventory) which is then sold and gives rise to accounts receivable. Thus, the core of asset investment in the firm is in the fixed asset section of the balance sheet.

The firm's fixed assets include three fairly general categories, although these categories may be subdivided into more detailed accounts. The first category is *land* which, of course, is part of the real estate property that has been acquired by the firm. One of the important characteristics of land in terms of financial planning is that it may not be depreciated. This is the only fixed asset for which this rule applies. The second category is *buildings*. Again, these are real estate assets in that they include office buildings, manufacturing facilities, warehouses, and other facilities. The third general category is *equipment*, a very general classification that may include manufacturing equipment, rolling stock (trucks, railcars, etc.), and office equipment.

Notice that Horizon Technology has a total of $430 million invested, at cost, in fixed assets. According to generally accepted accounting principles, these assets are recorded at original cost and may not be written up even if they should increase in value. Instead, with the exception of land, they will be written down over a specified period of time. The *accumulated depreciation* account (which appears immediately below the total original cost of fixed assets) is the method by which the accounts have been written down. The accumulated depreciation account is the sum of all depreciation expense that has been taken over the life of the assets to date (excluding land). *Net fixed assets* is the difference between gross fixed assets and accumulated depreciation. In the case of Horizon Technology, net fixed assets amount to $265 million, bringing total assets to $515 million.

Capital budgeting is the process by which decisions concerning fixed asset investments are made. The process will address not only *how much* should be invested in fixed assets but also the *proper mix*. The mix will vary for different firms. Typically, a manufacturing firm will have a large investment in buildings, equipment, and perhaps land. A professional services firm may have less invested in equipment and buildings if the majority of its facilities have been leased. While it is difficult to generalize the proper mix of fixed assets for any firm or industry, the techniques that are used in capital budgeting can be easily adapted to all cases. Thus, it is not necessary for a firm to have invested exactly as Horizon Technology in order for capital budgeting concepts to be applied.

Liabilities and Equity

The liabilities and equity sections appear on the right hand side of the balance sheet. As in the asset section, liabilities are listed in order of liquidity. The liability that will be paid first is listed first. In this case, this is *accounts payable*, a short-term liability that is often associated with the inventory account. Such liabilities often arise through purchases of inventory and represent future payments to vendors. The management of accounts payable is frequently accomplished by considering the cost of financing through vendors versus obtaining short-term financing in other respects. Accounts payable is an important source of finance that is used by manufacturing and service firms alike.

Accrued expenses do not have a formal relationship to another account on the balance sheet. Instead, accrued expenses are those associated with expenses that have been incurred but not billed, for example, accrued taxes or accrued payroll.

On the other hand, the next liability, *notes payable* is contractual in nature. Frequently, notes payable arise from bank relationships and are notes payable to the bank. Notes payable can be used to finance not only short-term activities of the firm, such as inventory purchases, but also longer-term activities such as fixed-asset acquisitions. Thus, notes payable can be either short-term or long-term. Restrictive covenants will often apply, some of which will actually impact decisions about the acquisition or disposal of fixed assets. Again, this is an example of the way in which capital budgeting decisions are linked to other operational and financial aspects of the firm.

Long-term debt is the fourth liability and can take a number of forms. One of these is debentures which are unsecured bonds, that is, bonds that have no assets of the firm that collateralize them. However, the absence of assets to secure long-term debt does not imply that these liabilities have no restrictions. Debentures often have clauses or restrictive covenants in their indentures that restrict the extent to which the firm can change its mix of fixed assets over time or the extent to which the firm may dispose of fixed assets. The indenture is the agreement between the issuer of a bond and the purchaser of a bond as to the terms and conditions that will govern the financing arrangement. On the other hand, a mortgage bond is an example of a secured bond with fixed assets of the firm as collateral. Again, there is a close tie between the financing of assets, in many cases, and decisions about the assets themselves.

The capital budgeting decision may not be viewed in isolation but must be considered in its totality. Particularly in the case of notes payable and long-term debt, liabilities are sources of funds that are often used to acquire fixed assets and the decision maker must be aware of any applicable considerations associated with them.

The bottom right-hand section of the balance sheet is the equity section. The claims reflected here do not have contractual terms such as interest or principal payments. Instead, preferred and common stock equity of the firm represents indefinite claims on the firm.

Common stock is a residual claim on the firm, i.e., all other claims have priority. As a result of this ranking, the common stock holder typically will require the highest rate of return among all providers of capital to the firm that are reflected on the right-hand side of the balance sheet. While the debt holder, bond holder, or bank note holder will expect interest payments and eventual principal repayment, the common stock holder does not have a claim to specific, fixed payments. Instead, the common stock holder is paid dividends that are variable in amount instead of being set contractually. These dividends are declared by the firm's board of directors. The process generates uncertainty for common stock shareholders. Unlike their bondholding counterparts, common stock shareholders receive what remains after interest payments and all other expenses are paid. Even then, the amount and timing of their distributions depend on the actual dividend declaration by the board of directors. It is this uncertainty, along with the residual position within the firm, that causes the common stock holder to require a much higher rate of return than other claimants on the firm.

Accordingly, the rate of return that is required by the common stockholder must be considered when making fixed asset acquisition decisions. If the earnings that are generated by fixed assets are insufficient to meet the expectations of shareholders, then the projects will not only be disappointments but will also lead to more difficulty in subsequently raising capital. Again, the fixed asset acquisition decision is linked to the expectations of current stock holders as well as the firm's ability to raise funds in the future.

Preferred stock is a hybrid between the common stock and the long-term debt of the firm. Preferred stock does not mature (as do bonds), but preferred stock does receive a dividend (as does common stock). Unlike common stock dividends, however, preferred stock dividends are typically fixed in amount (as in the case of bonds). So preferred stock shares some attributes of both – there is a stream of level payments but the payments do not end at some predetermined date.[2] Because preferred stock receives

---

[2] The exception to this rule is the less common limited-life preferred stock.

a fixed payment (and a higher priority than common stock), the cost of this capital must also be considered in capital budgeting decisions.

All providers of capital must be satisfied as illustrated by the balance sheet configuration of Horizon Technology. The left-hand side of the balance sheet represents the investments of the firm and, in the case of Horizon, these investments are heavily concentrated in fixed assets because it is a manufacturing firm. The right-hand side of the balance sheet demonstrates that the sources of funds for these investments are related to a number of claimants on the firm – debtholders, preferred stock holders, and common stock holders. In the case of Horizon, a large percentage of the funds derive from equity funds. This is true of most companies that are not financial corporations. Non-financial corporations typically have roughly half of their assets financed by debt and the remainder by equity.[3]

The Income Statement

Figure 1.2 shows a consolidated income statement for Horizon Technology Company. Again, this is a typical income statement, although numerous subcategories may exist within each line item.

The first line of the income statement is *sales*. In this case, sales are generated by the revenue-generating operations of the company. Since this is a manufacturing firm, the fixed assets enable the firm to create products and that inventory is sold. The sales are reflected at retail prices and reflect a markup over cost. The actual mix of sales and products is directly tied to the fixed asset configuration of the firm (referring again to the balance sheet). Thus, it is fixed assets that enable this firm to create the inventory that gives rise to sales, some of which are shown in accounts receivable. Again, the sales level is directly tied to decisions with respect to fixed asset investments, making fixed asset acquisitions a critical element of the decision-making process of the firm.

---

[3] The actual mix of debt and equity in a firm will depend on the country, as some countries have more reliance on debt financing as opposed to debt, especially bank debt.

FIGURE 1.2

Horizon Technology Co. Consolidated Income Statement* 1998

Sales	$197
Variable costs	(79)
Gross margin	118
Fixed cash expenses	(35)
Depreciation	(13)
Net operating income	70
Non-operating income	5
Non-operating expense	(2)
Earnings before interest and taxes	73
Interest expense	(15)
Earnings before taxes	58
Income taxes	(20)
Net income	$ 38
Preferred stock dividends (8%)	$ 4
Income available to common stock holders	$ 34

* In millions of dollars.

Variable costs are the second line of the income statement. These include such items as the labor that is necessary for production, the raw materials that go into producing the item, and supplies. While other items may also be included in variable costs, labor and raw materials essentially are the primary components of variable costs. In some cases, a portion of overhead is considered variable – for example, the amount of electricity that must be used to run a line during production.

The actual cost of production will be directly tied to the fixed asset acquisition decision. For example, some equipment may facilitate the use of high technology that keeps variable costs low. Such equipment, however, may have a higher acquisition cost than a less high-tech alternative. The capital budgeting decision must incorporate the consideration of the costs as well as revenues.

The difference between sales and variable costs is *gross margin*, or the dollar amount that the operations of the firm have generated for a particular period – in this case the year 1998 – which can then help cover fixed expenses, required payments to preferred shareholders, and ultimately dividend payments to common shareholders.

Before any dividends may be paid, however, *fixed cash expenses* must be covered. These include recurring costs that do not vary with production levels. For example, if facilities are leased, the lease payments do not depend on the level of production or sales. Another example of fixed cash expense is management salaries which typically do not vary with production, as do production labor costs.

The next line of the income statement is actually not a cash outflow at all. *Depreciation* is an allocation for the period (in this case, 1998) of the past costs of acquiring fixed assets. Depreciation expense is therefore a non-cash expense. But because depreciation provides a tax shield, it is important in the appropriate selection of fixed asset acquisitions. This means that depreciation represents a write-off against income that reduces taxes, but not a cash outflow in the amount of the expense. The extent to which a project provides such a tax shield is a critical element of capital budgeting.

The difference between gross margin and fixed expenses is *net operating income*. This is effectively the income generated by the firm's asset base. In this case, Horizon Technology Company derives $70 million in income for the year on a base of $515 million in assets. More specifically, the $265 million in fixed assets produced $70 million for the firm during 1998.

The next two line items on the income statement reflect the non-operating, incidental income and expense of the firm. For example, *non-operating income* may be interest income received on a temporary investment in securities. As a technology manufacturing firm, Horizon is not engaged principally in securities investment, but may have set aside funds temporarily when it had temporary excess liquidity. Any income generated in this and other ways will be reflected in non-operating income. Similarly, *non-operating expenses* are those expenses that typically are not incurred in the normal course of business for Horizon Technology. An example of a non-operating expense might be brokerage fees associated with purchasing and selling the temporary investments mentioned earlier.

The difference between net operating income and non-operating income and expense is *earnings before interest and taxes* (EBIT). Thus, EBIT is largely associated with the operations of the firm, but can include a small amount of non-operating income and expense. For most firms, it is reasonable to consider net operating income as virtually equal to EBIT. Throughout this book, the assumption is that the two are equal.

The next line item on the income statement is *interest expense*. Interest expense is directly tied to the amount of debt that the firm has incurred. Notice that interest expense is listed before income tax is computed. Interest expense is tax deductible, while dividend payments are not. Interest expense in this case is $15 million on a debt base of $65 million in notes payable and $150 million in long-term debt. Notes payable cost Horizon Technology 6.5% per year and long-term debt 7.5% for a total of $15 million in interest expense.

The net of all the above-mentioned items is *earnings before taxes*. For Horizon Technology, this amount is $58 million. Income taxes (federal, state, and local, as applicable) are based on taxable income. In a GAAP-prepared set of financial statements, earnings before tax is the equivalent of taxable income.[4] In this case, Horizon has computed a $20 million tax liability on a taxable income of $58 million, leaving *net income* of $38 million.

Notice that the $38 million will be distributed to preferred and common stock holders. Preferred stock dividends of $4 million will be paid at a flat rate of 8%. Notice that the rate of 8% for preferred stock is higher than the rate of interest for either noteholders or bondholders as is typically the case. Preferred stock holders expect to receive a higher rate of return because their priority is lower than noteholders and bondholders.

---

[4] GAAP is the acronym for generally accepted accounting principles. Differences between accounting for tax purposes and accounting for book purposes (GAAP) can cause differences between taxable income and earnings before tax.

Moreover, preferred stock holders will be paid only when sufficient income remains after interest payments.

This leaves $34 million available to common shareholders, which amount may or may not be used to pay dividends. This decision is the responsibility of the board of directors. Another important issue in capital budgeting is the extent to which future earnings available to common shareholders will be retained in the firm to finance fixed asset acquisitions. Any retention of future earnings to pay for capital projects should not be considered costless. Essentially, shareholders permit the firm to retain earnings to the extent that the funds are reinvested in projects for which shareholders will earn at least the rate of return available on their next best investment alternative. This concept of *opportunity cost* is central to the idea of the firm's cost of capital, the minimum required rate of return that is acceptable in selecting capital projects.

As illustrated here, the income statement and the balance sheet give insight into the necessary considerations for decisions with respect to fixed asset acquisitions. All of these elements are included in the approaches and techniques of capital budgeting.

MAXIMIZING SHAREHOLDER WEALTH

Simply stated, the objective of management is to maximize shareholder wealth. This goal is no less relevant for a member of a financial management team or an operational team that gives input to the fixed asset acquisition process.

The Concept

The concept of maximizing shareholder wealth is straightforward in theory, but can become complicated in implementation. Shareholder wealth is tied to the value of the firm itself. In turn, the value of the firm can be viewed either as the long-term value of the firm as an ongoing concern or as the value of the firm when it is broken apart into its operational components. The value of the firm should be linked with the concept of shareholder wealth. Difficulties in the decision-making process arise when this linkage does not exist. The process breaks down when shareholder wealth is considered only in terms of the financial proceeds that can be generated in the short term. The integrity of the process is maintained as long as the value of the firm is seen as a proxy for the value of shareholder wealth. Thus, the assumption of intrinsic value firm as an ongoing operation underlies the discussions throughout this book.

The Constraints

Figure 1.3 illustrates certain constraints to maximizing shareholder wealth even when shareholder wealth maximization is linked with the continued viability of the firm. In the context of a corporation, the decision-making process among managers can be complicated. When the interests of all the stakeholders (shareholders, employees, general public) are considered, it can become even more involved.

FIGURE 1.3

Constraints to Shareholder Wealth Maximization

Agency costs
- Management incentives
- Short-term versus long-term perspective

Creditors
- Protecting employees
- Satisfying short-term liabilities
- Bondholder interests

Social responsibility
- Avoiding externalities

The decision-making process is constrained by certain considerations:

- agency costs
- creditors
- social responsibility.

Agency costs arise because the decisions that are made within the firm are made *on behalf of* shareholders, but often not *by* shareholders. Instead, corporate management makes decisions for shareholders. Agency costs arise when the incentives that are in place for managers lead them to make decisions that are not consistent with either the long-term viability of the firm or the maximization of shareholder wealth.

Such problems can be associated with the incentives or compensation packages for management. Some compensation packages are based on achieving and maximizing quarterly profits and do not compensate for the strength of the firm in its market, increasing market share, technological advances, or employee development. Nevertheless, these activities improve the firm and help it to be viable over the long term. Thus, management incentives are key to containing the potentially detrimental effects of this agency relationship. One of the ways to mitigate any such damage is to provide for management incentives which encourage managers to view the firm from the same perspective as shareholders. This can be accomplished by compensating management with common stock. To the extent that the value of the firm increases (as evidenced by its stock price), management compensation increases.

Another approach is to monitor the actions of managers periodically. The premise is that managers will make fewer decisions that are not in line with the best interests of shareholders if they know their actions are being monitored. The monitoring itself often takes the form of auditing, with the most common form being the annual review of financial statements by outside auditors or certified public accountants (CPAs). Increasingly, internal audits are also being performed – of both the financial and operational results. Both external and internal audits help to reduce the agency costs associated with the separation of ownership and management.

The second constraint in maximizing shareholder wealth is one that should legitimately be maintained. The claims of *creditors*, as discussed earlier in this chapter, have a higher priority than those of shareholders. Accordingly, creditor interests must be protected. Without this constraint, it is possible to construct a scenario in which shareholder wealth could be maximized by selling all assets of the firm and making a large cash distribution to shareholders. This would effectively leave creditors with no assets to generate earnings to honor the payments promised to them. The contractual arrangements between the firm and its creditors often reflect this vulnerability and the need to protect creditors. Some of the most important creditors of the firm are its employees. To protect these claimants, there are often certain rules under liquidation procedures in a country's legal system that give priority to unpaid wages in the event of a liquidation. These laws often also protect unpaid pension liabilities by giving such claims a special priority. Thus, the employees are considered one of the major creditors of the firm whose interest will be protected in the event of a liquidation.

In addition to employees, other claimants also receive protection. For example, short-term notes will contain a clause that net working capital (current assets minus current liabilities) may not fall below a certain amount. Alternatively, the current ratio (current assets divided by current liabilities) may not fall below a certain level. These clauses help to ensure that asset liquidation will not occur without legal recourse for providers of short-term funds.

Long-term providers of capital, such as bondholders, have equivalent rights and these are contained in the legal agreement between bond issuers and bondholders, called the *indenture*. These documents also contain provisions with respect to working capital and current ratios. Restrictive covenants may also stipulate that fixed assets, or some proportion of fixed assets, may not be sold without prior advice and approval of the bondholders. These restrictive covenants give management some flexibility in making fixed asset acquisition decisions and do not constrain the normal operations of the firm. At the same time, they do prevent a wholesale liquidation of the firm without the advice and consent of the bondholders. It is interesting to note that, while obligations to employees are protected by laws, the rights of bondholders must be written into the indenture. For this reason, indentures are often quite detailed so as to include every relevant consideration.

The third constraint to shareholder wealth maximization is *social responsibility*. This issue also involves protection of the legitimate rights of other parties. Basically, a company has a social responsibility not to create an *externality*, that is, not to incur a cost that is then passed on to another party. A firm creates an externality, for example, when it pollutes a river by dumping toxic by-products of production. The river pollution is a cost that is not absorbed by the company but by all those individuals that have access to and use the river. Companies may not create such externalities. Companies must also take responsibility for damages associated with the design and manufacture of their products.

There is a whole body of law that enforces this social responsibility on corporations that either provide a service or manufacture a product. At times, these laws may act as a constraint to shareholder wealth maximization. Nevertheless, they represent legitimate concerns and protective measures that have been devised to respond to the concerns.

Agency costs can – and should – be contained. The rights of creditors must be observed. The obligation for social responsibility should be recognized. All of these are issues (not always easy to quantify) that are considered in the capital budgeting decision, and in the decision-making process for the firm as a whole as financial managers strive to maximize firm value, and, ultimately, shareholder wealth.

THE DETERMINANTS OF FIRM VALUE

The value of the firm is based on some of the same fundamental concepts that are reflected in the financial statements. The first is that firm value is a function of asset value, liabilities, and equity as a residual. Figure 1.4 illustrates several asset valuation concepts. According to generally accepted accounting principles (GAAP), asset value that is included in the balance sheet of a firm will typically be based on *historical cost*. In terms of evaluating potential capital budgeting projects, historical cost has limited benefit. Historical cost is a way to keep track of what has been spent in the past and how those costs have been allocated over time. Thus, historical costs have some accounting applicability but very little relevance for strategic decision making or for decisions relative to the value of assets in an ongoing business context.

One of the reasons that this concept has so little applicability in a capital budgeting context is that book value does not reflect increases in asset value. Another problem with historical cost is that it is stated net of

---

FIGURE 1.4

Asset Valuation Concepts

Book value
- Historical cost
- Net of accumulated depreciation

Replacement value
- Supply and demand
- Technological implications

Value of future cash flows
- Ongoing concern
- Functional implications
- Interactions with other assets
- Long-term perspective

---

accumulated depreciation, a contra-asset account that increases over time. Thus, the book value of an asset approaches zero over time. Using book value to evaluate projects or to give an indication of the advisability of a future project is not well advised.

The second concept that might be considered is *replacement value*, that is, the cost that must be incurred to exactly replace the technology and capability. Essentially, market conditions will dictate this value. The actual use of a piece of equipment or property is not reflected in the replacement value. The primary considerations are supply and demand of the item in question and the extent to which it represents current technology. In some cases, a piece of equipment may not be the most technologically advanced version. In other words, it may have been succeeded by one or two generations of improvements and, because of this, its market value may be quite low. On the other hand, if this equipment is used in connection with a revenue-generating project, the replacement value has little relevance. What is more important is how its use will contribute to the larger picture.

The most important consideration with respect to a project is its effect on the firm's future cash flows. Thus, the capital budgeting decisions should be made not in the context of historical cost calculations for an asset, nor in the context of replacement value for fixed assets, but instead on the basis of an ongoing concern that will use the asset to generate cash flows. An example may be useful to illustrate. Suppose that a piece of equipment has an extremely high market value but no productive use within the firm. Such an asset should not be evaluated at its high market value but rather in terms of the minimal positive impact it will have on the firm's cash flow.

The first step, then, is to consider an asset in the context of the on-going firm. The second is to evaluate the functional aspects of the asset – not its historical cost or replacement value – and related cash flows. The third step is to consider the interaction of the asset with the other assets or activities of the firm. If the equipment will increase productivity or reduce expense, it has a positive interaction with other assets.

EARNINGS, STOCK PRICE, AND CAPITAL BUDGETING DECISIONS

There is a direct relationship between the capital budgeting decision and the market price of the firm's stock. More specifically, earnings, stock price, and capital budgeting decisions are interrelated as illustrated by Figure 1.5 in the case of Horizon Technology. The price of Horizon's common stock is currently $28 per share. With 8.5 million shares outstanding, this company has a total market capitalization (total value of equity) of $238 million. This common stock market capitalization can be compared with the book value of equity as reflected on the balance sheet (see Figure 1.1 on page 5). According to the consolidated balance sheet, the common equity of Horizon Technology totals $235 million while the market capitalization is $238 million.[5] This implies a slight premium of market over book value for Horizon Technology.

The relationship also follows for per-share comparisons, which is a more frequently used approach. The earnings per share that are available to Horizon's common shareholders is $4–$34 million available (see Figure 1.2 on page 12) divided by 8.5 million shares. Since the stock is selling at

---

FIGURE 1.5

Horizon Technology Co. Common Stock Price Analysis

Stock price per share	$28
Stock outstanding	8.5 million shares
Market capitalization	$238 million
Earnings per common share	$4
P/E ratio	7
Implied required return on investment	0.143

---

[5] Book value of common equity is the total of common stock ($85 million) and retained earnings ($150 million).

$28 while its earnings per share is $4, this implies a price-to-earnings or P/E ratio of 7. This means that the market is willing to pay seven times the earnings level for essentially the future prospects of continued, ongoing operations. This ratio also provides some insight into the required return for Horizon Technology by the market. For this reason, there are important capital budgeting implications.

The returns for a shareholder are generated in two forms. Shareholders receive dividend payments and they also realize capital gains or losses.[6] Thus, the rates of return to a shareholder are composed of dividend yield and capital gains yield. Assuming for a moment that the capital gains yield is related essentially to the market's projection of growth for the firm, the dividend yield has a much shorter term prospective.

$$\text{Dividend yield} = \frac{D_1}{P_0}$$

As can been seen in the above equation, the dividend yield is the expected dividend for the coming period as a percentage of the current market price of the stock. If a no-growth situation is assumed, the dividend yield becomes effectively the total return to the shareholder. The no-growth scenario is based on an assumption that all earnings are paid to shareholders as dividends. In this case, the dividend yield becomes earnings per share as a percentage of price, or the inverse of the P/E ratio. Thus, in a no-growth situation, the inverse of the P/E ratio is the required return to a shareholder.

Using this approach, the implied required rate of return on investment from the perspective of common shareholders of Horizon Technology, is 14.3% as shown in Figure 1.5. In the context of capital budgeting decisions, this 14.3% rate of return must be incorporated into the cost of capital used to fund projects. If those projects that are accepted do not return at least 14.3% to equity holders, the market will discount the value of new and existing stock for all shareholders. Hence, there is a close link

---

[6] Capital gains and losses are increases and decreases in the market value of an asset.

between the capital budgeting decision and changes in shareholder wealth. Any perceived errors in capital budgeting decisions will cause the stock market to devalue the stock.

The interaction between the capital market for financial assets and the real market for tangible assets cannot be dismissed lightly. It is necessary to identify elements that are relevant for a project decision and then to incorporate market information with considerations internal to the firm. Capital budgeting decisions are closely tied to the shareholder wealth maximization.

CHAPTER 2

HOW PROJECTS ARE CLASSIFIED

Introduction

By Function: Expansion, Replacement, and R&D

How Proposed Projects Can Affect Other Projects

Analysis of Announced Projects

INTRODUCTION

Should a project that improves an existing process be evaluated in the same way as one that takes the firm into a completely different area of business? The answer clearly is "No," but how does the analysis change? How is the analysis altered when the company can adopt only one of several alternatives? These questions suggest that project analysis must begin with appropriate categorization of the alternatives. This chapter considers various approaches to project classification.

It should be noted that project ideas are generated in a number of ways – not necessarily with a mind to classifying them in any particular fashion. For example, the executives of the firm – including representation from marketing, production, and finance – may identify markets in which the firm should compete. The same process may yield product ideas that fit the strategic plans of the company. Likewise, a firm with appropriate incentives may benefit from the insights of all employees. For example, if the incentives system is well structured, potentially profitable project concepts may as easily be generated in the field by marketing specialists or by the technical employees who are involved in the manufacturing process.

Once the project ideas are generated – from whatever source – it is important to structure their analysis in a way that is cost-effective. The process of evaluation is not without cost. Proper classification can enhance the efficiency of evaluation.

Recall the four projects announced in mid-1998 and introduced in Chapter 1.

■　■　■

UK independent oil and gas explorer, Hardy Oil and Gas PLC, announced a decision to invest *£95 million* by the end of 1998 and *£300 million* by 2002 in order to increase production by a projected factor of five.

■　■　■

South African Vodacom, entered a contract to purchase *$75 million* of mobile-telephone base station equipment as part of a *$489 million* capital expenditure to expand capacity.

■　■　■

US-based Sprint Corporation announced that its new integrated, on-demand network would cost less than *$400 million* over a two-year period.

■   ■   ■

In Latvia, Sodra of Sweden and Metsae-Serla Oy of Finland appeared on the verge of being selected to enter a joint venture with the Latvian government to construct a state-of-the-art wood pulp mill for *$1 billion*.

■   ■   ■

These decisions help to illustrate the classification concepts that follow.

BY FUNCTION: EXPANSION, REPLACEMENT, AND R&D

Capital projects may be classified in certain basic ways. With respect to *function*, the five primary classifications are:

- expansion
- replacement
- regulatory
- research and development
- other.

Expansion projects are those that enable the firm to engage in:

- *expansion of existing products or markets*; or
- *expansion into new products or markets.*

When a company expands existing products or markets, it is frequently involved in creating new outlets or distribution channels. In these cases, the company must attempt to accurately assess demand for its product or service. Expansion into new products or markets involves strategic considerations for the firm, a long-term perspective, and (typically) substantial investment of resources.

Expansion projects are, in a sense, the most risky because they represent previously unexplored areas. Because of this, expansion projects will generally be evaluated using a relatively high minimum required rate of return. At the same time, an expansion project may also offer substantially higher rewards than other projects.

A *replacement* project may be one of two types

- *maintenance of business*; or
- *cost reduction*.

A maintenance-of-business replacement decision is common because of normal wear and damage to equipment used in production of goods and services. In many cases, the most relevant considerations are whether the firm should continue to produce the goods or services and, if so, whether the existing facilities should continue to be used. If the answer to these questions is "Yes," the maintenance-of-business replacement decisions require relatively little analysis – perhaps no more than competitive bids from several vendors.

When the replacement decision involves a cost reduction potential, the existing equipment may still be serviceable. However, if existing facilities are obsolete, profits into the future will be depressed unnecessarily. Thus, a more detailed analysis of cost and benefits is required. Examples of cost savings include, but are not limited to, reduction of required cost input components, reduction of waste or spoilage, reduction of variable labor costs, or improvement of the quality of the finished product.

A *regulatory* project is one that complies with a law or set of regulations. In this sense, the social responsibility constraints mentioned in Chapter 1 have considerable relevance in making regulatory project decisions. In many cases, for example, environmental agencies establish guidelines for clean air and clean water. Any projects undertaken must comply with these guidelines. Regulatory projects are not pursued in order to maximize shareholder wealth but rather to comply with a standard of performance set by a governmental body. The normal approach of maximizing shareholder wealth by analyzing cash flows and looking to the firm's long-term viability has less applicability for a regulatory project. The primary consideration is to incur a minimal cost for responsible compliance.

Research and development (R&D) projects are essential to ensure the long-

2

term viability of many firms, particularly if the firm is involved in technological products and services. At the same time, the revenues associated with the expense of R&D projects is often difficult to estimate and, at best, realizable only at some future date. Also, these projects often require sizable investments. The combination of uncertainty as to incremental cash inflows and high levels of investment cause R&D projects to be considered among the most risky type of capital project.

Other projects include those that are not easily classified in the above-mentioned categories. These include office space and other capital projects not directly associated with the sales of the firm.

HOW PROPOSED PROJECTS CAN AFFECT OTHER PROJECTS

In addition to being classified by their actual function, capital projects may also be classified in terms of their relationship to each other.

FIGURE 2.1

Classifying Capital Projects by their Relationship to other Projects

Independent

$$V_A + V_B = V_C$$

Mutually exclusive

$$V_A + V_B = V_A \text{ or } V_B$$

Interrelated

$$V_A + V_B < \text{ or } > V_C$$

where V_A = Value of Project A

V_B = Value of Project B

V_C = Sum of V_A and V_B

In this respect, the three classifications are:

- independent
- mutually exclusive
- interrelated.

Independent Projects

Independent projects are those that can be adopted without affecting the adoption of other projects. Figure 2.1 illustrates that Project A and Project B are two projects that can be valued independently. The value of these projects is indicated by V_A and V_B. When two projects are independent, it is possible to do one of the following.

1 Accept A and reject B.
2 Reject A and accept B.
3 Accept both.
4 Reject both.

In the event that both projects are accepted, the firm will realize a total value that is the simple or linear combination of their individual values. As indicated in Figure 2.1, when the two projects are independent, the value of $V_A + V_B = V_C$, where V_C is the numerical summation of the value of the two projects.

Mutually Exclusive Projects

On the other hand, if the two projects are *mutually exclusive*, it is not possible to accept both. If Project A is accepted, $V_B = 0$. Likewise, if B is accepted, $V_A = 0$. An example of a mutually exclusive situation is the development of a piece of land that is suitable for either a hospital or a hotel. The land may not be used for both. If the hotel is accepted, the hospital must be rejected. Conversely, if the hospital is accepted, the hotel must be rejected.

Interrelated Projects

Independent and mutually exclusive projects are the extreme of project classification in terms of the relationship of projects to each other. *Interrelated* projects are somewhere between these two extremes in that they will have some impact on other projects, but will not preclude their acceptance. An example of interrelated projects is the situation in which one may impact the market share of the other. For example, if Project A is a new, small automobile and Project B is a mid-sized model, both may be accepted and manufactured. However, the possibility exists that part of the potential customer base for the small automobile may be attracted to the medium-sized automobile. These projects are interrelated because the revenues of one could reduce the revenues of the other. In this case, the value of $V_A + V_B$ will be less than V_C.

It is also possible that projects can have a synergistic relationship in the sense that they complement each other. For example, Project A may involve the manufacture of computer hardware while Project B focuses on the design of computer software. If both projects are adopted, the combined sales revenue may be greater than the sum of the revenues of the individual projects when they are adopted without the other. In this case, $V_A + V_B$ is greater than V_C. Because of these interactions, interrelated projects are the most difficult to evaluate.

These general classifications are useful in establishing certain rules of decision making. They will be used to help identify the relevant types of cash flows and other factors that are important in the capital budgeting decision.

ANALYSIS OF ANNOUNCED PROJECTS

A sample of capital expenditure announcements was noted earlier in this chapter (and also in Chapter 1). As might be guessed, each of these large projects is an expansion project, implying significantly more risk than a cost-reduction replacement project or a maintenance replacement project. However, each has somewhat different implications for the company involved.

In the case of the *UK* independent oil and gas explorer, Hardy Oil and Gas PLC, much of the *£300 million* to be spent by 2002 will be devoted to a new form of exploration. The new technology will enable Hardy to process the oil and gas output on the floor of the sea instead of at the surface. This efficiency is expected to enable the firm to capitalize on oil fields that would otherwise have been uneconomical to develop.

South African Vodacom plans to spend its *$489 million* to expand coverage, capacity, and performance of its network. As such, it will increase the distribution of an existing product.

US-based Sprint Corporation has committed its roughly *$400 million* over a two-year period in order to enter a new product line that will integrate services now being offered to customers by a number of vendors – local telephone carriers, long-distance telephone carriers, Internet access providers, and cable television services.

The *Latvian* project in which Sodra of Sweden and Metsae-Serla Oy of Finland are involved is an expansion project that will take both companies into markets in which they have not previously operated.

CHAPTER 3

CAPITAL BUDGETING TECHNIQUES

INTRODUCTION

A number of "tools" have been developed to assist the financial manager in selecting the appropriate combination of investments for the firm. The techniques range considerably in complexity. The descriptions below begin with the simplest (and oldest) of them. Definitions are given first, followed by fuller descriptions and numerical examples. In each case, the technique is applied, in a world of certainty, to a hypothetical Project A that has a relatively simple cash flow pattern, an initial cost of $1,000 with four annual cash inflows of $300, $500, $400, and $300.

	0	1	2	3	4
Project A	(1,000)	300	500	400	300

The capital budgeting methods are:

- payback period
- accounting rate of return
- internal rate of return
- net present value
- profitability index.

Definitions

Payback Period

The expected length of time for positive cash flows to equal the initial cost, or the time it is expected to take to recover the initial investment.

Accounting Rate of Return (ARR)

The average contribution of the project to the net income of the firm as a percentage of the initial cost or average book value of the project.

Internal Rate of Return (IRR)

The rate of return that causes the cost of the project to equal exactly the present value of the future cash flows.

Net Present Value

The difference between the present value of the future cash flows (using the appropriate discount rate) and the initial cost of the project.

Profitability Index (PI)

The ratio of the present value of the future cash flows (using the appropriate discount rate) and the initial cost of the project.

PAYBACK PERIOD

Most Intuitively Appealing Approach

The payback period is the oldest method of evaluating capital projects and the easiest to apply. To illustrate this technique using Project A, consider cash flows required "to cover" the initial investment and the balance of the cost that is "unrecovered" on a period-by-period basis.

	0	1	2	3	4
Project A	(1,000)	300	500	400	300
To cover		300	500	200	–
Unrecovered	1,000	700	200	–	–

Fully 100% of the cash flows of years 1 and 2 are required to recover the initial investment. Only 50% of the cash flow of year 3 is required to complete covering the initial investment. Thus, the payback period is 2.5 years.

The payback period is an intuitively appealing approach in that it is easy to understand. It also has the advantage of giving some insight to the estimated time during which the initial investment will be "at risk."

Problems Associated with Payback Period

Notice that there are certain theoretical shortcomings of the payback period:

■ the cash flows which occur after the initial investment has been recouped are ignored;

- the time value of money is not considered.

To fully appreciate the significance of these theoretical problems, suppose that two other projects, X and Y, were mutually exclusive (as defined in Chapter 2) and had the following expected cash flows.[1]

	0	1	2	3
Project X	(100)	75	25	1,000
Project Y	(100)	25	75	50

Project X has a payback period of two years, as does Project Y. Using this criterion alone, a firm would be indifferent between the two. Yet, it is obvious, by inspection, that Project X is superior to Project Y. In year 1,

Project X has a cash flow three times that of Project Y. While this rela-tionship is reversed in year 2, the time value of money causes the two-year cash flow pattern of Project X to have a higher value than that of Project Y. The danger of ignoring post-payback period cash flows is highlighted in year 3. The $1,000 associated with Project X makes the project *clearly* superior to Project Y. But the payback period result is not at all sensitive to the Year 3 cash flows.

Using *discounted* cash flows improves the technique, theoretically, by incorporating the time value of money. Assuming a discount rate of 10%, the valuation of Project A cash flows at Period 0 is given in Figure 3.1. These cash flows are also shown below to facilitate the explanation. The *discounted* payback period is 3.07 years, since the $13.52 required in year 4 is 7% of that year's discounted cash flow.

	0	1	2	3	4
Project A	(1,000)	272.73	413.22	300.53	204.90
To cover		272.73	413.22	300.53	13.52
Unrecovered	1,000	727.27	314.05	13.52	–

---

[1] When two projects are mutually exclusive, the acceptance of one of the projects results in the non-acceptance of the other(s). That is, only one of the available alternatives may be accepted.

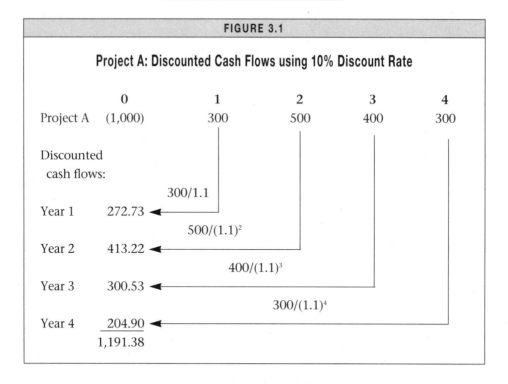

FIGURE 3.1

Project A: Discounted Cash Flows using 10% Discount Rate

	0	1	2	3	4
Project A	(1,000)	300	500	400	300

Discounted
 cash flows:

		300/1.1
Year 1	272.73	
		$500/(1.1)^2$
Year 2	413.22	
		$400/(1.1)^3$
Year 3	300.53	
		$300/(1.1)^4$
Year 4	204.90	
	1,191.38	

Even using discounted cash flows, however, the focus of this method is the recovery of initial cost. Cash flows after the payback period are never considered. This remains then, the most theoretically troublesome aspect of the payback period technique of project evaluation.

ACCOUNTING RATE OF RETURN

The *accounting rate of return* (ARR) is the second oldest capital budgeting method. The incremental effects of a project on the firm's balance sheet form the basis for the computation. Essentially, the accounting rate of return is similar to a number of other rates of return that measure income as a percentage of investment. The specific income measure is average cash flow less depreciation expense. The investment measure is either initial cost of the project or average projected book value.

$$ARR = \frac{\left(\dfrac{\sum\limits_{t=1}^{n}(CF_t - Dep_t)}{n}\right)}{I} \tag{1}$$

$$ARR = \frac{\left(\dfrac{\sum\limits_{t=1}^{n}(CF_t - Dep_t)}{n}\right)}{ABV} \tag{2}$$

where   ARR   =   accounting rate of return

CF_t = net cash flow in year t

Dep_t = depreciation expense in year t

n = expected number of years of project life

I = initial project investment

ABV = average book value of project

= average cost – accumulated depreciation.

Note that equation 2 includes the effect of depreciation in the denominator, while equation 1 does not. Assuming straight-line depreciation with a zero salvage value, the ARRs for Project A are given in Figure 3.2. (See Chapter 4 for a discussion of depreciation methods.)

Using initial investment as the denominator, ARR is 12.5%. Using average book value, the result is 25%. Both results depend on the method of depreciation used. If a form of accelerated depreciation had been used or if a non-zero salvage value had been assumed, the rates of return could have been significantly different.

However, sensitivity to depreciation method is not the primary deficiency of this capital budgeting technique. Like the payback period method, the accounting rate of return does not consider the timing of cash flows. For this reason, it should not be relied upon as the exclusive evaluation tool.

FIGURE 3.2

Project A: Accounting Rate of Return

Income and Book Value

	0	1	2	3	4
Project A	(1,000)	300	500	400	300
Depreciation[1]		(250)	(250)	(250)	(250)
Income[2]		50	250	150	50
Book value[3]	1,000	750	500	250	–

Averages

Income[4]	$125
Book value[5]	500

Accounting Rates of Return

Using initial investment:

$$\frac{125}{1000} = 0.125$$

Using book value:

$$\frac{125}{500} = 0.25$$

[1] $Dep_t = (Cost - Salvage\ value)/n$
[2] Income = Cash flow – Depreciation expense
[3] Book value = Cost – Accumulated depreciation
[4] Average income = (50 + 250 + 150 + 50)/4 = 125
[5] Average book value = (1,000 + 750 + 500 + 250 + 0)/5 = 500

INTERNAL RATE OF RETURN

Unlike payback period and accounting rate of return, the *internal rate of return (IRR)* is a function of both the amount of the cash flows *and* their timing. As noted in the Introduction, the IRR is that rate of return which causes the present value of the future cash flows to exactly equal the initial cost of the project. In applying the IRR technique, the objective is to find the rate that will satisfy this condition.

$$I_0 = \sum_{t=1}^{n} \frac{(CF_t)}{(1 + IRR)^t} \tag{3}$$

Measuring Expected Rate of Return

Again we will use Project A to develop the concept of IRR or the expected rate of return of a project. In Figure 3.1, 10% does not appear to be Project

A's IRR. The IRR causes the present value of future cash flows to exactly equal the initial investment. In this case, at 10%, the sum of the present value of future cash flows is $1,191.38, *not* $1,000. The appropriate adjustment at this point is to try a discount rate that is higher than 10%.[2]

If 20% is chosen, the present value of the future cash flows is $973.36, as can be seen in Figure 3.3. Since the resulting present value is $26.64 less than the initial cost, a lower discount rate should now be used. Using 18%, the present value of the future cash flows is $1,011.53, $11.53 more than the initial cost (Figure 3.3). This rate is too low because the present value of future cash flows still exceeds the initial investment. However, it is a better estimate than 20% (since the difference between present value and initial cost is smaller using 18%). This process – attempting one rate, making adjustments as needed – is referred to as *trial and error*.

The exact IRR of Project A is 18.59%. Any financial calculator that is programmed to accept unequal cash flows can be used to obtain this result.

Shortcomings of IRR

The internal rate of return is an improvement over payback period and accounting rate of return, but it is not without theoretical shortcomings. The first is that all interim cash flows are assumed to be reinvested at the IRR. Figure 3.4 illustrates the effect of this reinvestment assumption. Project A cash flows are first assumed to be reinvested at the project's IRR of 18.59%, resulting in a terminal value of $1,977.88.[3] The entire project has now been reduced to two values – a cost of $1,000 and a terminal

---

[2] Since the present value of any single amount is that amount multiplied by $\frac{1}{(1+k)^t}$ increasing the discount rate will decrease the present value.

[3] Since the point of valuation (on the time line) is now the end of the fourth year, the value of the year 4 cash flow is unaffected by compounding. The cash flows of years 1, 2, and 3 are compounded for 3, 2, and 1 years, respectively, or for the number of periods that elapse between the cash flow and the point of valuation. See Appendix A for a full discussion of compounding (and discounting) rules.

FIGURE 3.3

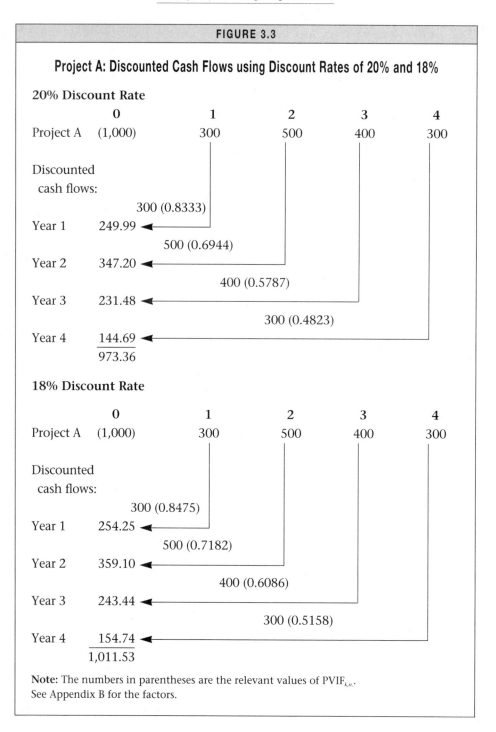

Project A: Discounted Cash Flows using Discount Rates of 20% and 18%

20% Discount Rate

	0	1	2	3	4
Project A	(1,000)	300	500	400	300

Discounted
  cash flows:

300 (0.8333)

Year 1   249.99 ◄

500 (0.6944)

Year 2   347.20 ◄

400 (0.5787)

Year 3   231.48 ◄

300 (0.4823)

Year 4   144.69 ◄
          973.36

18% Discount Rate

	0	1	2	3	4
Project A	(1,000)	300	500	400	300

Discounted
  cash flows:

300 (0.8475)

Year 1   254.25 ◄

500 (0.7182)

Year 2   359.10 ◄

400 (0.6086)

Year 3   243.44 ◄

300 (0.5158)

Year 4   154.74 ◄
          1,011.53

Note: The numbers in parentheses are the relevant values of $PVIF_{k,n}$.
See Appendix B for the factors.

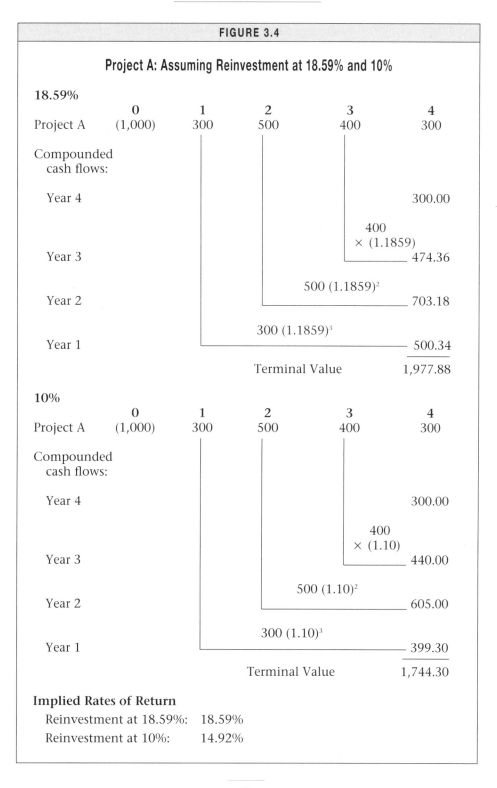

FIGURE 3.4

Project A: Assuming Reinvestment at 18.59% and 10%

18.59%

	0	1	2	3	4
Project A	(1,000)	300	500	400	300

Compounded
cash flows:

Year 4   300.00

$400 \times (1.1859)$

Year 3   474.36

$500 (1.1859)^2$

Year 2   703.18

$300 (1.1859)^3$

Year 1   500.34

Terminal Value   1,977.88

10%

	0	1	2	3	4
Project A	(1,000)	300	500	400	300

Compounded
cash flows:

Year 4   300.00

$400 \times (1.10)$

Year 3   440.00

$500 (1.10)^2$

Year 2   605.00

$300 (1.10)^3$

Year 1   399.30

Terminal Value   1,744.30

Implied Rates of Return

Reinvestment at 18.59%:	18.59%
Reinvestment at 10%:	14.92%

value of $1,977.88. The implied rate of return can be found through the future value formula described in Appendix A.

$$FV_n = PV(1 + k)^n \qquad (4)$$

The resulting rate is 18.59%.[4] When the reinvestment rate equals the IRR, the implied rate of return equals the IRR.

The impact on implied rate of return of assuming a 10% reinvestment rate is also shown in Figure 3.4. In this case, the terminal value of $1,744.30 yields an implied rate of return of 14.92%, considerably lower than the project's internal rate of return. *To the extent that the IRR differs significantly from the firm's true reinvestment opportunities, the IRR does not accurately reflect the rate of return of the project in question.* This is a fundamental difficulty with using the internal rate of return as a decision model. This problem can be mitigated, however, by establishing a reasonable reinvestment assumption, finding the terminal value under this assumption, and calculating the implied rate of return, as in Figure 3.4.

The second caveat with respect to using IRR is that, in some instances, there may be more than one IRR, or more than one rate that causes the cost to equal the present value of the future cash flows. This situation will only arise when the algebraic sign of all *future* cash flows is not positive, i.e., if the signs of the cash flows change more than once. Project A, as specified above, is *not* such a project.[5]

A frequently cited example of a project with two IRRs is a high-speed crude oil pump that costs $1.6 million, called Project P for this example. In the first year, the oil pump will generate $10 million more in revenue

---

[4] $1,977.88 = 1,000(1 + k)^4$

$$k = \left(\frac{1,977.88}{1,000}\right)^{\frac{1}{4}} - 1$$

$$k = \quad 0.1859$$

[5] Descartes' rule of signs suggests that there may be one root – or IRR – for each change in sign of the cash flows. Project A has only one change in sign, therefore, only one IRR.

than the current pump. However, in the second year, it will generate $10 million less because the oil reserve will be depleted. The net cash flows for this Project P are as follows.

	0	1	2
Project P	(1.6)	10.0	(10.0)

The discount rates of 25% and 400% will cause the cost of the project to exactly equal the present value of the future cash flows. Clearly, such a result makes analysis difficult since *both* rates satisfy the criterion of the internal rate of return. To overcome this problem, the cash flows may be adjusted to cause the project to have a more conventional pattern.

One approach to accomplish a more traditional cash-flow pattern is to *find the terminal value using an estimate of the firm's reinvestment rate*, as described above. If 10% is chosen, the value of the year 1 cash flow at year 2 is $11 million [$10 million × (1.10)]. When this amount is added to the year 2 cash flow of negative $10 million, the net result is a positive $1 million in year 2. Project P's implied rate of return when $1.6 million is invested currently to receive $1 million in two years is a negative 20.9%.[6]

Alternatively, the negative year 2 cash flow can be discounted to year 1 and added to the year 1 cash flow, again, to determine the implied rate of return. When this approach is taken, the result is a negative 43.2%.

$$k = \left(\frac{\left(\frac{-10}{1.10} + 10 \right)}{1.6} \right) - 1 \qquad (5)$$

$$= -0.43218$$
$$\cong -43.2\%$$

---

[6] $1,000,000 = 1,600,000(1 + k)^2$

$\frac{1,000,000}{1,600,000} = (1 + k)^2$

$\left(\frac{1,000,000}{1,600,000} \right)^{\frac{1}{2}} - 1 = k$

$k = -0.2094 \cong 20.9\%$

As illustrated by this example, the two approaches can lead to significantly different results. But, without adjustment of the cash flows, the meaning of multiple IRRs is, at best, ambiguous.

NET PRESENT VALUE

Net present value (NPV) is a technique that overcomes the deficiencies noted in the other methods, for the following reasons.

- *Cash flows*, not income measures, are the basis for the calculation, overcoming problems associated with the accounting rate of return.
- *All cash flows* are considered unlike the IRR approach.
- The *time value of money* is recognized, overcoming the deficiencies of payback period and the accounting rate of return.
- There is no *assumption that interim cash flows are reinvested at the project's internal rate of return.*

Measuring Direct Impact on Shareholder Value

Net present value is the difference between the present value of the future cash flows and the initial investment.

$$\text{NPV} = \left(\sum_{t=1}^{n} \frac{\text{CF}_t}{(1 + k)^t} \right) - \text{I}_0 \tag{6}$$

Central to the determination of net present value is the appropriate discount rate, k. This rate should reflect investors' rate of return on the next best investment alternative. As such, k is a minimum required rate of return for the project. Conceptually, the bracketed term in equation 6 represents the *value* of the project to the firm. The initial investment, I_0, is the required cash outlay to obtain the project. If the value of the project exceeds the required cash outlay, value is added to the firm, which, in turn, increases shareholder wealth.

Since maximization of shareholder wealth is the objective of financial management, the measurement of change in shareholder wealth that is directly attributable to specific projects makes net present value a decidedly useful technique. When project value is more than the initial investment, an increase in shareholder wealth can be realized if the project is adopted. When the reverse is true – that is, the project value is less than the initial investment – adoption of the project will lead to a decrease in shareholder wealth.

It should be noted that, if the value of the project exactly equals the required investment, the project earns exactly the minimum required rate of return and is, therefore, desirable. This assertion can be intuitively supported with a simple example. Suppose that you have decided that the appropriate rate of return for a given project is 10%. Suppose further that the project has an initial cost of $100 and has one future cash flow in the amount of $110 to be received in one year. At 10%, the present value of the future cash flow is $100. Since the initial cost is also $100, this project has a zero net present value. The project provides exactly the required rate of return. Hence, if you consider this project undesirable, this implies that your required rate of return is *greater than* 10%. Thus, projects with net present values of zero are acceptable.

The NPV of Project A at a discount rate of 10% can be readily determined by reference to Figure 3.1. NPV is the summation of discounted future cash flows less the initial investment. The present value of the four future cash flows of Project A is $1,191.38, the initial investment is $1,000. Therefore, the NPV is $191.38. At 10%, adopting Project A will add $191.38 to the wealth of shareholders.

The Relationship Between NPV, Discount Rate, and IRR

A lower discount rate would increase NPV, while a higher rate would have the opposite effect.[7]

- As k increases, NPV decreases or approaches zero.
- The rate that will cause NPV to equal zero, is the project's IRR. (Recall that IRR is that rate which causes the present value of the future cash flows to exactly equal the initial investment. When this condition is satisfied, the difference between value and cost (NPV) is zero.)
- At discount rates higher than IRR, the value of the project is less than the initial investment and NPV is negative.

If 10% is the shareholders' opportunity cost, Project A's IRR of 18.59% compares favorably to this rate. Even its implied rate of return of 14.92%, assuming a 10% reinvestment rate (see Figure 3.4), is higher than the required return of 10%. As noted above, its value exceeds its cost by $191.38. When independent projects are being considered, IRR and NPV techniques will yield consistent results. If the IRR is greater than the required return, NPV will also be greater than zero. (See Chapter 2 for a description of project classifications.)

PROFITABILITY INDEX

The profitability index (PI) is related to NPV. NPV is the *difference* between project value and cost. Profitability index is the *ratio* of project value to cost.

$$PI = \frac{\sum_{t=1}^{n}\left(\frac{(CF_t)}{(1+k)^t}\right)}{I_0} \qquad (7)$$

---

[7] Changes in discount rate change the value of a project, but do not change its cost.

Notice that profitability index is as sensitive to discount rate as is NPV. At 10%, the PI of Project A is 1.19.

$$PI = \frac{1,1191.38}{1,000} \tag{8}$$

$$= 1.19138$$

Since PI measures value of the project per dollar of initial investment:

- PI will be greater than 1 whenever the value of the project exceeds its cost.
- If cost and value are equal, PI will equal 1.
- PI will be less than 1 if the value of the project is less than its cost.

INDEPENDENT PROJECTS

As long as independent projects are being considered, the application of IRR, NPV, and PI will yield comparable results. If IRR exceeds required return, NPV will exceed zero, and PI will exceed one. When IRR equals required return, NPV equals zero, PI equals one. Similarly, when IRR is less than the appropriate discount rate, NPV will be negative, while PI will be less than one.

MUTUALLY EXCLUSIVE PROJECTS AND RESOLVING CONFLICTING RANKINGS

As noted in Chapter 2, mutually exclusive projects must frequently be evaluated. Project B is a second hypothetical project with a four-year life.

	0	1	2	3	4
Project B	(650)	250	250	250	250

FIGURE 3.5

Mutually Exclusive Projects A and B: Comparison of Capital Budgeting Techniques

Cash Flows

	0	1	2	3	4
Project A	(1,000)	300	500	400	300
Project B	(650)	250	250	250	250

Capital Budgeting Methods

	Project A	Project B
Payback period (years)	2.5	2.6
Accounting Rate of Return		
Initial cost (%)	12.5	13.5
Book value (%)	25.0	27.0
Internal Rate of Return (%)	18.59	19.77
Net Present Value @ 10% ($)	191.38	142.48
Profitability Index @ 10%	1.19138	1.21919

The results of applying the capital budgeting techniques is given in Figure 3.5. The payback period of Project A is marginally shorter than that of Project B, while the accounting rates of return of Project A are lower than Project B's. Thus, using the payback period, the proper ranking is Project A first, Project B second. But the ARRs suggest the opposite ranking.

Since payback period and ARR are sub-optimal techniques (because cash flows after the payback period are ignored and, generally speaking, differences in the timing of cash flows are not recognized), more emphasis should be placed on the IRR and NPV results. As has already been noted, both projects have an IRR well in excess of 10%, the presumed opportunity cost of investors. But the projects are mutually exclusive, and must be ranked. Using IRR, Project B, with an IRR of 19.77%, dominates Project A, with an IRR of 18.59%.

However, the NPV of Project A is $191.38, while that of Project B is $142.48, suggesting that Project A dominates. So which project is preferable? Recall that, in order to earn the internal rate of return, interim cash flows must be reinvested at the IRR, and that net present value calculations measure the change in shareholder wealth associated with a given project. Since the next best investment alternative is assumed to be 10%, it appears inappropriate to assume reinvestment at a rate almost twice 10%. Assuming reinvestment at 10%, the implied rates of return of Project A and Project B are 14.92% (see Figure 3.4) and 15.59%, respectively, still suggesting dominance of Project B. The rate of return of Project B is calculated below, assuming that each of the $250 cash flows can be reinvested at 10%.

$$k = \left(\frac{FV}{PV} \right)^{\frac{1}{n}} - 1$$

$$= \left(\frac{250(FVIFA_{(0.10,4)})}{650} \right)^{\left(\frac{1}{4}\right)} - 1$$

$$= \left(\frac{250(4.641)}{650} \right)^{\left(\frac{1}{4}\right)} - 1 \qquad\qquad (9)$$

$$= (1.785)^{\left(\frac{1}{4}\right)} - 1$$

$$= 0.1559 = 15.59\%$$

But the net present value of Project A is $48.90 greater than that of Project B ($191.38 – 142.48). This apparent contradiction can be resolved in one of two ways. The first involves identifying the difference in net cash flows between the projects. This difference is specified in Figure 3.6 as Project Z, and involves $350 in initial investment, with annual cash flows ranging from $50 to $250. The NPV of Project Z is $48.91[8], its IRR 16.37%, and its

---

[8] Difference is because of rounding.

FIGURE 3.6

Mutually Exclusive Projects A and B: Analysis of Difference in Cash Flows

	0	1	2	3	4
Project A	(1,000)	300	500	400	300
Project B	(650)	250	250	250	250
Project Z					
(difference)	(350)	50	250	150	50

Project Z

NPV @ 10% ($)	48.91
IRR (%)	16.37
PI	1.13974

---

profitability index is 1.14. Project Z is a project which should be undertaken even if Project B is selected. But accepting both Project B *and* Project Z is equivalent to accepting Project A.

The second manner in which this conflict can be resolved is by reference to the profitability index. At first glance, it appears that Project B dominates Project A using this criterion since $PI_B = 1.22$, while $PI_A = 1.19$. However, the initial investment of the two projects is significantly different. If Project B is selected, the $350 not required for investment in real assets will likely be invested in the capital market at the rate of 10%, since this is the next best investment alternative. As noted above, when the expected return equals the required return, a project's profitability index will be equal to 1. On a weighted average basis, Project A is the more desirable alternative.

$$PI_A = \left(\frac{1,000}{1,000} \right) (1.19) = 1.19 \tag{10}$$

$$PI_B = \left(\frac{650}{1,000} \right) (1.22) + \left(\frac{350}{1,000} \right) (1.00) = 1.14 \tag{11}$$

Investing $650 in Project B and $350 in the next best investment alternative implies receiving value of $1.14 per dollar invested, while investing $1,000 in Project A yields $1.19 for each dollar invested. Clearly, Project A is preferable. Thus, net present value and the profitability index (when evaluated on a weighted average basis) will lead to the correct decisions with respect to mutually exclusive projects.

3

SUMMARY

All capital budgeting techniques seek to establish some minimum performance for projects, below which the project becomes unacceptable. This minimum performance is then compared to the project's expected performance. When the projects are mutually exclusive, the objective is to select the project that exceeds the minimum acceptable performance by the widest margin.

Rates of return (IRR and ARR) are commonly the focus of such evaluations. While the terms and the calculations may vary, two themes are common to all such analyses – required and expected rates of return. In the context of examples in this chapter, required return has been represented by the capital market interest rate (opportunity cost). In either case, the required rate of return is established by reference to considerations external to the project itself and represents what the project rate of return *should be*.

On the other hand, expected return is a function of only the project cash flows. The internal rate of return is the rate that causes the cost to equal the present value of future cash flows. The accounting rate of return is a function of initial investment, future cash flows, depreciation method, and estimated life of the project. Nothing external to the project is considered. Every expected rate of return is an estimate of what the project return *will be*.

This logic extends to all the techniques that have been discussed. Figure 3.7 summarizes the relevant decision criteria and is a convenient reference in applying the capital budgeting methods. However, the assumptions underlying the measurements and other theoretical issues discussed above must be considered to interpret the results properly and to arrive at appropriate investment decisions.

Essentially, financial managers should select those projects that earn at least the opportunity cost of investors. Identifying these projects is the objective of a number of analytical methods – payback period, accounting rate of return, internal rate of return, net present value, and profitability index. Net present value and profitability index are superior to the others in theoretical construct. Furthermore, net present value is a direct measure of the change in shareholder wealth that may be attributed to a specific project. Whichever technique is used, however, a potential capital project will be acceptable only if its expected performance is at least equal to the minimum required performance as establishment by the firm's management.

FIGURE 3.7

Capital Budgeting Techniques: Decision Criteria

	Independent Projects		Mutually Exclusive Projects
			Select Projects with
	Accept	Reject	
Payback period	$PP_I \leq PP_R$	$PP_I > PP_R$	Shortest PP, given $PP_I \leq PP_R$
Accounting rate of return	$ARR_I \geq ARR_R$	$ARR_I < ARR_R$	Highest ARR, given $ARR_I \geq ARR_R$
Internal rate of return	$IRR_I \geq k$	$IRR_I < k$	Highest IRR, given $IRR_I \geq k$
Net present value	$NPV \geq 0$	$NPV < 0$	Highest NPV, given $NPV_I \geq 0$
Profitability index	$PI \geq 1$	$PI < 1$	Highest PI, given $PI_I \geq 1$

I = project being considered
R = minimum acceptable (required) performance
k = minimum required rate of return on cash flows

3

RELEVANT CASH FLOWS

Introduction

■

General Themes in Cash Flow Analysis

■

Analyzing Expansion Project Cash Flows

■

Additional Cash Flows for Replacement Decisions

■

Depreciation

■

Expansion Project Example

■

Replacement Project Example

■

Summary

INTRODUCTION

The examples of capital budgeting techniques in Chapter 3 used net cash flows as a basis for each analysis. Typically, these cash flows have several components – i.e., the cash flow for each year is composed of a number of elements. This chapter explains the components of net cash flow for each year in the useful life of a capital project. In general, the relevant cash flows are:

- cost
- installation
- working capital changes
- incremental revenue
- cost savings
- incremental expense
- depreciation tax shield
- salvage value
- cash flows that are unique to replacement decisions
- forgone depreciation tax shield of existing project
- forgone salvage value of existing project
- sale of existing project.

After each of these components is explained, numerical examples of an expansion project and a replacement are covered. In these examples, the capital budgeting techniques introduced in Chapter 3 are illustrated.

GENERAL THEMES IN CASH FLOW ANALYSIS

As listed in Figure 4.1, there are four *overriding themes* in the determination of appropriate cash flows for capital budgeting analyses.

FIGURE 4.1

Cash Flow Considerations for Capital Budgeting Projects

- Cash flow versus income

- Incremental cash flows

- After-tax cash flows

- Net annual cash flows

Actual Cash Flow

The first theme is the concept of *cash flow* as contrasted with the concept of income. Income is an accounting concept that matches revenues with expenses in the appropriate manner for each accounting period. Accounting income often includes items that do not represent actual cash flow – notably depreciation. Because of this, all elements of a capital budgeting analysis must be considered in actual cash flow terms. Any non-cash items must be adjusted. In most cases, the primary difference between accounting income and cash flow is depreciation expense.

Depreciation is an allocation of previous cost to appropriate time periods. This typically involves large purchases of equipment, buildings, and other facilities that have been acquired in prior periods. Because these capital expenditures bring benefits to the firm over a long term, their cost appropriately is allocated over their useful life.[1] Each year's depreciation repre-

---

[1] The exception to this general rule is accelerated depreciation, as permitted by many national tax codes. In these cases, the tax code is used to encourage capital investment because capital investment leads to job growth and higher economic standards.

---

sents a non-cash expense for the firm. In order to convert net income to cash flow, depreciation expense is added to income. The same adjustment is made for the amortization of other intangible assets such as goodwill, patents, or copyrights. Generally, whenever there is a non-cash element in income, it must be added back to arrive at the cash flow that ultimately is the basis for capital budgeting analyses.

At the same time, depreciation has important tax consequences because it reduces taxable income. In turn, the reduction of taxable income creates a reduction in tax liability. Furthermore, since depreciation is often a large expense category, the reduction in tax liability associated with depreciation expense makes this category an important part of the analysis of a potential capital expenditure.

Incremental Cash Flows

In constructing a capital budgeting analysis, gross (or total) cash flows are not relevant. Instead, the critical cash flows are *incremental cash flows* – those that measure the differential impact of a project on the overall cash flow stream of the firm. For example, if a new piece of equipment is being considered for the manufacture of a new product, the relevant revenue cash flow is the change in revenue that can be realized. In every cash flow category, the appropriate cash flow to be included is incremental cash flow.

After-tax Cash Flows

The impact of each cash flow on the firm's tax liability must also be considered. In all cases, the cash flows must be stated on an *after-tax basis*. The adjustment for taxes will vary depending on the nature of the item in question. Some cash flows have no impact on tax liability. Others are fully taxable or tax-deductible. Still others are only partially taxable or tax-deductible. Each cash flow must be analyzed to establish the correct tax treatment.

FIGURE 4.2		

Cash Flow Analysis

Type	Typical Timing	After-Tax Cash Flow
Cost:		
Purchased (C)	0	$-C$
Transferred (OC)	0	$-OC$
Installation (INST)	0	$-INST$
Working capital changes (WC):		
Increase	0	$-WC$
Increase-reversal	n	WC
Decrease	0	WC
Decrease-reversal	n	$-WC$
Revenue increase (REV)	1 through n	$REV(1 - t)$
Cost savings (CS)	1 through n	$CS\,(1 - t)$
Increased expense (EXP)	1 through n	$-EXP(1 - t)$
Depreciation tax shield:		
Net project (DTS_n)	1 through n	$(Dep_t)(t)$
Existing project (DTS_E)	varies	$-(Dep_t)(t)$
Salvage value:		
New project (SV_n)	n	$SV_n + (BV_n - SV_n)(t)$
Existing project (SV_E)	varies	$-SV_E + (BV_E - SV_E)(t)$
Sale of existing project (MV_E)	0	$MV_E + (BV_E - MV_E)(t)$

Net Annual Cash Flows

Once individual cash flows for a given year (or other period) have been identified and stated on an after-tax basis, they must be aggregated to arrive at the *net annual cash flows* that may be attributed to a capital budgeting project. These net annual cash flows correspond to the amounts used in Chapter 3 to illustrate the capital budgeting techniques of payback period, accounting rate of return, internal rate of return, net present value, and profitability index. Generally, the life of the project should be analyzed in terms of the time of acquisition (time zero) and the years of useful life of the project (years 1 through *n*). In addition, the last year of useful life may have associated with it special cash flows related to project disposal.

ANALYZING EXPANSION PROJECT CASH FLOWS

Figure 4.2 is a summary of the individual cash flow components that must be considered in each capital budgeting decision. All of the elements may not apply, but to the extent that an item is relevant it should be included in the analysis, stated on an after-tax basis.

Cost

The first cash flow in Figure 4.2 is *cost*. This is the purchase price or the market value of the project. Typically, it will be purchased at time zero and there will be no tax impact at the time of acquisition because the cost of capital equipment may not be written off at the time of acquisition. Instead, the cost is written off over the life of the equipment or over some alternative period of time.

If the equipment has been transferred from another division in the company, the appropriate cost to be included is the *opportunity cost* of using that equipment in another capacity. This notion of opportunity cost corresponds to that discussed in Chapter 3 – the minimum required rate of return is the investor's next best alternative investment outside the firm. In a similar way, the opportunity cost of transferred equipment is its value in the next best application.

Notice that these after-tax cash flows – cost or opportunity cost – are associated with a negative sign. This is appropriate because the impact of purchasing equipment or of devoting a piece of previously-owned equipment to a new use will be to reduce cash. In the analysis format that is demonstrated in this chapter, the cost of purchased or transferred equipment will always be associated with the negative sign, as will other items that reduce cash. Other items will have a positive sign and will be netted against negative cash flows to arrive at net annual cash flows.

Installation

Like the acquisition cost, the cost of *installation* for a piece of equipment or other capital budgeting project may not be written off at the time of acquisition. Instead, the cost of installation is added to the purchase price and depreciated over the same period of time as the initial purchase price.

Working Capital Changes

Working capital requirements sometimes change when projects are adopted or technologies change. A working capital *increase* has the same impact on cash as the acquisition itself, that is, negative. On the other hand, once the project is concluded that commitment in working capital is no longer necessary. This means that the amount of the working capital increase at time zero (time of acquisition) is reflected as a negative and then reversed at time *n*.

As with the cost of acquisition and installation, there is no tax impact associated with working capital increases (or decreases). The after-tax cash flow is the same as the before-tax cash flow. For example:

- accounts receivable are deferred cash receipts after sale and give rise to no tax write-off, unless they are not collected;

- inventory is charged against income as cost of goods sold – after the actual sales occur.

If working capital requirements actually *decrease*, the impact on cash is positive. A working capital reduction is equivalent to reducing an asset through sale or other liquidation – creating a positive impact on cash. Once a project is completed, i.e., at time n, the efficiencies associated with the project presumably are no longer available and there should be a reversal (negative sign) in exactly the same amount.

It should be noted that over the life of the equipment, the new working capital levels are maintained through normal operational cash flows. For example, in reporting income, revenues are reduced by the *cost of goods sold* and this part of revenues is assumed to be reinvested in replacement of inventories (necessitating no further investment by the firm). For capital budgeting purposes, it is only necessary to reflect increases or decreases in working capital when the levels actually change. If the new working capital levels – established in the year of acquisition – are to be maintained throughout the project's useful life, there will be no further working capital cash flows until the reversal at the end of the project's life.

Incremental Revenues

Often capital projects are undertaken because increases in *revenue* are anticipated. Increases in revenue often mean sales increases or other forms of revenue enhancements. Unlike the capital cost of equipment and working capital changes, revenues are taxable. The after-tax cash flow (ATCF) is simply the revenue itself minus the taxes that are involved, where the taxes equal revenue (REV) multiplied by the tax rate (t).

$$ATCF = REV - REV(t) = REV(1 - t) \qquad (1)$$

The adjustment for taxes that is shown in equation 1 is the adjustment for any cash revenue, or expense. Essentially the adjustment then for a cash revenue or expense is to multiply that item by the quantity $(1 - t)$.

Cost Savings

In some cases, *cost savings* will accrue when a new technology or other equipment is adopted. These savings will be realized over the life of the project. They will result in higher net operating results for the firm, that is, more taxable income. Thus, for cost savings the appropriate adjustment is, again, to multiply the cost savings by the quantity $(1 - t)$.

Incremental Expense

It is also possible that a new project can cause additional *expense* for the firm. This may be increased maintenance expense or increased labor to operate equipment that requires a specialized labor pool. In any event, this is an expense that generally will be deductible. A cash expense should also be adjusted by multiplying it by $(1 - t)$. Because it is an outflow, that is, will have a negative impact on cash, it is associated with a negative sign as shown in Figure 4.2.

Depreciation Tax Shield

While capital equipment cannot be written off at the time of acquisition, it may be written off over its life. As noted above, the cost will be reflected as a negative in its entirety at time zero. The depreciation will occur from period 1 through period n or over the depreciable life of the project, whichever is shorter, and will generate a *depreciation tax shield*.

Depreciation expense reduces taxable income. However, because there is no cash outlay associated with this expense and because the expense shields other income from taxation, the net impact on cash is positive. This relationship can be illustrated by considering equation 1 once again. Notice that the after-tax cash flow is the amount of the cash item, in this case revenue, multiplied by 1 (because 100% is received) but then reduced by the percentage of the item that will be paid as taxes. This essentially means that while 100% will be received, $t\%$ must be paid out as taxes.

If this same logic is applied to a cash expense, the result is essentially the same. When a higher cash expense is incurred, 100% is paid out by the firm but t% is received in the form of tax relief. Taking this concept of a cash expense one step further and applying it to depreciation expense – a noncash item – it is easy to see the effect on the cash flow of the firm.

$$ATCF = Dep(0 - t) = -Dep(t) \qquad (2)$$

Equation 2 shows:

- the after-tax cash flow associated with depreciation expense is the amount of the depreciation multiplied by the amount paid – zero in this case;
- although 0% is paid, t% still is received in the form of a tax benefit.

When this term is simplified, it is clear that the after-tax expense associated with depreciation is negative. *A negative expense is a revenue.* Thus, depreciation expense has a positive cash impact. The amount of the impact equals the amount of the depreciation expense multiplied by the appropriate tax rate.

Salvage Value

The amount of value that remains once a project or a piece of equipment has been completely used is called its *salvage value*. A project's salvage value must also be included in the cash flow analysis. The taxability of proceeds from sale of equipment differs from the taxability of other operational revenues. Unlike a revenue or expense, the sale of a capital asset may or may not be taxable. If there is a gain on the sale of equipment, there will be a tax liability associated with that sale. If there is a loss on the sale of capital equipment, there will be a net tax benefit. A capital loss can be used to reduce taxable capital gains.

$$ATCF = SV + Tax\ Impact = SV + (BV - SV)(t) \qquad (3)$$

Equation 3 shows that there are then two elements of the sale of capital equipment. One is the actual proceeds of the sale or the projected salvage value. The second element is the tax impact. Since taxes are computed only on the capital gain or capital loss, equation 3 shows that the capital gain or loss will be computed on the basis of the sale price of the equipment (SV), and the book value of the equipment (BV).

Notice that equation 3 will yield a positive tax impact if the book value exceeds the salvage value. In an accounting sense, when book value exceeds salvage value, there is a capital loss. However, losses are tax deductible. Capital losses create tax shields (similar to depreciation) and, thus, have a net positive impact on cash. When there is an accounting loss, the second term in equation 3 will be positive.

Conversely, if there is an accounting gain, i.e., salvage value exceeds book value, the second term in equation 3 will be negative. This situation implies an accounting gain that generates additional tax liability.

Whenever a capital asset is sold, the impact on cash can be appropriately determined and reflected by the second term in equation 3. Notice that when book value equals salvage value, there is neither a gain nor a loss. In this case, there will be no tax impact and the net, after-tax cash flow will be the amount of the proceeds from sale.

ADDITIONAL CASH FLOWS FOR REPLACEMENT DECISIONS

If the project being considered is a replacement project, there is already an *existing* piece of equipment or technology in place. Furthermore, if the existing project still has remaining useful life, there are three ways that its abandonment or sale can impact cash flows:

- forgone depreciation tax
- forgone salvage value
- sale of existing project.

Forgone Depreciation Tax Shield

In a replacement decision, an existing technology may have a remaining useful life and remaining depreciable base. If the new project under consideration is accepted at time 0, the existing equipment will be disposed of at time 0. This means that the depreciation expense that *could have been recorded* for the old equipment in subsequent years *will not be recorded*. Since recording depreciation generates a positive cash flow impact, *forgoing* depreciation (losing the deduction) has a negative cash impact. Figure 4.2 shows that the *forgone depreciation tax shield* associated with the existing equipment is computed in the same manner as that of the new project, but has a negative sign.

Forgone Salvage Value

In a replacement decision, not only does the company lose the opportunity to depreciate the existing equipment, but it also loses the opportunity to sell it at the end of its useful life. That is, the firm has a forgone cash flow associated with selling the existing project at some time in the future.

The *forgone salvage value* is calculated in the same way as the salvage value for the new, proposed project (see Figure 4.2). The difference is that the net after-tax cash flow has a negative sign because it represents a cash flow that will not be realized if the new, proposed project is accepted.

Sale of Existing

Should the new project be accepted, the existing technology or project will be sold at time 0 – the year of acquisition. The *sale of the existing* facilities is also the sale of a capital asset and is computed in the same way as the salvage value of the new project. This is also shown in Figure 4.2.

DEPRECIATION

The method that is used to depreciate capital assets will have an important impact on the cash flow analysis. The depreciation methods that are commonly used for tax purposes are straight-line and double-declining.

Depreciation Methods

The *straight-line* method of depreciation allocates an equal amount of expense for each year of the useful life of an asset.

$$\text{Dep}_t = \frac{(\text{Cost} - \text{SV})}{n} \tag{4}$$

The straight-line method involves a depreciable base that is determined by subtracting the projected salvage value from the cost. This depreciable base is then divided by the number of years of useful life that are projected for the project. This is the basic form of straight-line depreciation.

Double-declining depreciation involves adjusting the depreciable base each year, or more accurately, adjusting the percentage of the original cost that remains undepreciated each year. For example, in a double-declining depreciation approach to a five-year useful life, the annual straight-line percentage that is suggested is 20% of the depreciable base. Often, a half-year convention is adopted, with one-half of the normally allocated depreciation during the first year. For example, in the case of a five-year asset, using the double-declining approach the first year will be allocated two times the normal straight-line approach, that is, 40%. Under the half-year convention, the first year's depreciation percentage would be reduced to 20%. Having depreciated 20% in the first year, 80% remains to be depreciated.

For the second year, the 80% remaining amount is divided by the original useful life of the asset, that is, five years, producing 16% per year. Since it is the double-declining method, 32% of the depreciable base is taken in the second year. This leaves 48% of the original base to be depreciated over the remaining life (100% – 20% – 32%).

In the third year, the 48% is divided by five to arrive at a 9.6% straight line. Twice this percentage is 19.2%, and 28.8% remains undepreciated (100% – 20% – 32% – 19.2%).

This process continues until a pure straight-line method will permit a larger deduction. When the straight-line calculation produces a higher percentage depreciation rate, the remaining years are converted to straight-line, based on the remaining useful life.

Since one-half of the allowed depreciation is taken in the first year, the remaining half is added at the end of the useful life. For example, in the case of a 5-year double-declining method with half-year convention, depreciation will be spread effectively over 5½ years.

MACRS Classifications

Figure 4.3 illustrates the Modified Accelerated Cost Recovery System, often referred to by the acronym MACRS. This system is recognized by the US Internal Revenue Service (IRS) and is a useful example for all forms of accelerated depreciation. All of the depreciation schedules under MACRS are computed in the standard format using the double-declining method as described in the section above.[2] Figure 4.3 gives examples of those asset classifications that will be depreciated using an accelerated 3-, 5-, 7-, 10-, 15-, or 20-year schedule. Residential rental property may be depreciated over 27.5 years, non-residential real estate property over 31.5 years. All assets that do not have a specifically defined class life are assigned a seven-year class life and follow the seven-year depreciation schedule. The only exception to the double-declining method with half-year convention rule is real property. Residential rental property and non-residential real property are depreciated using a straight-line schedule, again, with a modification in the first year. The modification in the first year is not half-year

---

[2] Options using 150% of straight-line are available. In addition, certain large real estate property will be subject to something other than half-year convention. The IRS schedules provide specific provisions.

convention, but is instead a monthly convention that depends on the month in which the asset was placed in service.

FIGURE 4.3

Modified Accelerated Cost Recovery System (MACRS) Classifications

Property Class	Description
3-year	Tractor units for use over the road.
5-year	Automobiles, taxis, buses, trucks, computers and peripheral equipment, office machinery (typewriters, calculators, copiers, etc.) and any property used in research and experimentation.
7-year	Office furniture and fixtures (desks, files, etc.) and any property that does not have a class life and that has not been designated by law as being in another class.
10-year	Vessels, barges, tugs, similar water transportation equipment, any single purpose agricultural or horticultural structure, and any tree or vine bearing fruits or nuts.
15-year	Roads, shrubbery, wharves (if depreciable), and any municipal wastewater treatment plant.
20-year	Farm buildings and any municipal sewers.
Residential	Any real property that is a rental building or rental property structure (including mobile homes) for which 80% or more of gross rental income for the tax year is rental income from dwelling units. Depreciated over 27.5 years.
Non-residential	Any real property that is not residential rental real property. Depreciated over 31.5 years.

Note: Applies to tangible property placed in service after 1986.
Source: Internal Revenue Service, United States, publication 534: *Depreciation*.

MACRS Depreciation Schedule

Figure 4.4 shows the annual depreciation amounts that can be taken based on an asset's depreciable base in the USA for the class lives of 3 years through 20 years. Depreciation methods will vary by country and by asset class, but the principles are similar. Notice that beginning with the five-year class life, there is a conversion to straight-line at one point within the schedule. For 5-year class life that point is year 4; for 7-year class life, year 5; for 10- and 15-year class lives, year 7; and for 20-year class life, year 9. These percentages can be reconstructed following the same approach

FIGURE 4.4						
MACRS Depreciation Schedule						
Depreciation Rate (%)						
Year	3-year	5-year	7-year	10-year	15-year	20-year
1	33.33	20.00	14.29	10.00	5.00	3.750
2	44.45	32.00	24.49	18.00	9.50	7.219
3	14.81	19.20	17.49	14.40	8.55	6.677
4	7.41	11.52	12.49	11.52	7.70	6.177
5		11.52	8.93	9.22	6.93	5.713
6		5.76	8.92	7.37	6.23	5.285
7			8.93	6.55	5.90	4.888
8			4.46	6.55	5.90	4.522
9				6.56	5.91	4.462
10				6.55	5.90	4.461
11				3.28	5.91	4.462
12					5.90	4.461
13					5.91	4.462
14					5.90	4.461
15					5.91	4.462
16					2.95	4.461
17						4.462
18						4.461
19						4.462
20						4.461
21						2.231

described above in connection with the double-declining depreciation method.

EXPANSION PROJECT EXAMPLE

Figure 4.5 shows the details for a project that represents an expansion project. The assumption in this example is that a new piece of equipment will be necessary in order for the firm to expand into a new product line. The cost of this equipment is $200,000 and $20,000 is required for installation. The product and the equipment are both expected to have a useful life of ten years. At the end of this time, the anticipated salvage value is $10,000. Because this new equipment is not specified in the MACRS classification, it will be assigned a seven-year class life.

FIGURE 4.5	
Expansion Project: New Product Line	
Cost of equipment ($)	200
Installation cost ($)	20
Useful life (years)	10
Anticipated salvage value ($)	10
Depreciation method	MACRS
Class life (years)	7
Incremental annual sales ($)	53
Incremental annual expenses ($)	6
Working capital requirement increase ($)	15
Tax rate (%)	34
Note: Dollar amounts are in thousands.	

The product that will be produced by this equipment is anticipated to generate incremental annual sales of $53,000 per year before tax. This is the amount of sales over and above existing sales levels that can be expected. Incremental annual expenses that will be associated with the new product amount to $6,000 per year. In order to produce and support the product, increases in inventory and accounts receivable (working capital) will be required in the amount of $15,000. The firm's tax rate is 34%.

Because this product has an expected life of ten years but a class life of seven years, it will be depreciated over a period that is shorter than its expected life. The depreciation schedule that applies is shown in Figure 4.6. This corresponds exactly with the seven-year class life that is illustrated in Figure 4.4. In each year, the amount of $220,000 is multiplied by the appropriate rate.

4

FIGURE 4.6

Expansion Project: Depreciation Schedule

Year	Depreciation Rate	Amount (000s)
1	0.1429	31.438
2	0.2449	53.878
3	0.1749	38.478
4	0.1249	27.478
5	0.0893	19.646
6	0.0892	19.624
7	0.0893	19.646
8	0.0446	9.812

Note: Total cost to be depreciated is $220,000, including installation.

Notice that the percentages sum to 1 and that the amounts in the depreciation amount column total exactly $220,000. This means that over the roughly 7½ year period for which depreciation will be taken, all of the tax basis for this equipment will be depreciated. By the end of the eighth year, the book value of this asset will be zero. When the asset is sold at the end of its useful life, all of the proceeds will be taxable because the entire proceeds will represent a capital gain, that is, an amount greater than the book value of zero.

FIGURE 4.7

Expansion Project: Net Annual Cash Flows*

Year	0	1	2	3	4	5	6	7	8	9	10
Cost	(200)										
Installation	(20)										
WC	(15)										15
Revenue[1]		34.98	34.98	34.98	34.98	34.98	34.98	34.98	34.98	34.98	34.98
Expense[2]		(3.96)	(3.96)	(3.96)	(3.96)	(3.96)	(3.96)	(3.96)	(3.96)	(3.96)	(3.96)
DTS[3]		10.69	18.32	13.08	9.34	6.68	6.67	6.68	3.34		
Salvage value[4]											6.6
	(235)	41.71	49.34	44.10	40.36	37.70	37.69	37.70	34.36	31.02	52.62

* In thousands of dollars.

[1] $REV(1 - t) = 53 (1 - 0.34) = 34.98$

[2] $EXP(1 - t) = 6 (1 - 0.34) = 3.96$

[3] $DTS_t = Dep_t(t) = Dep_t(0.34)$ (see also Figure 4.6.)

[4] $SV = SV_N + (BV_N - SV_N)(t) = 10 + (0 - 10)(0.34) = 10(1 - 0.34) = 6.6$

78

Net Annual Cash Flows – Expansion Project

The identification of annual cash flows for this expansion project are presented in Figure 4.7. In the year of acquisition (year zero), the cost, necessary installation cost, and working capital increases must be recognized. Net cash flow in year zero is negative $235,000.

The revenues for this project are consistent for each of the years given. Notice that this is a simplifying assumption that can be easily adjusted in the likely event that the project has uneven cash flow increases over the life of the project. For example, it would be a simple matter to modify the cash flow analysis to incorporate a higher revenue stream in the first few years with a lower revenue stream to be realized in the later years. In other words, the cash flows for each year can be easily tailored to the actual expectations of management. Because the revenues are actual cash receipts, the adjustment to arrive at after-tax cash flow is to multiply the $53,000 amount by $(1 - 0.34)$. This yields an after-tax incremental revenue stream of $34,980.

Annual expense is also expected to increase. These amounts are reflected in the analysis with negative signs on an after-tax basis. Again, the necessary adjustment to arrive at the after-tax expense is to multiply the $6,000 by the quantity $(1 - 0.34)$. The net incremental annual expense will be $3,960.

The depreciation tax shield is the amount of depreciation multiplied by the tax rate. Because the depreciation expense varies for each year, the depreciation tax shield will also vary.

The salvage value is the last item that is considered in Figure 4.7. It is based on the actual anticipated salvage value plus the tax impact. The tax impact is the difference between anticipated book value and anticipated salvage value, multiplied by the tax rate. In this case, 100% of the anticipated salvage value will be taxable. That means that the entire amount of proceeds from sale of the asset will be taxable. As a result, the after-tax cash flow associated with the salvage value is computed in the same way that any other 100% taxable cash receipt would be computed – by multiplying it by $(1 - t)$. In this case, the after-tax cash flow associated with the salvage value is $6,600.

Cash Flow Analysis – Expansion Project

Figure 4.8 illustrates the application of payback period, internal rate of return, net present value and profitability index for the expansion project analyzed in Figure 4.7. In the case of the payback period, after five years, only $21,790 remains to be recovered of the initial cash flow. This amount is 58% of the net cash flow for year 6. Thus the payback period is 5.6 years using gross cash flows. If discounted cash flows were used to compute the payback period (i.e., if discounted payback period was computed), the payback period would be slightly longer because each cash flow would contribute slightly less to cover the initial cost.

FIGURE 4.8

Expansion Project: Cash Flow Analysis*

Payback period (years)	5.6[1]
Internal rate of return (%)	11.8
Net present value[2] ($)	34.52
Profitability index	1.15[3]

*In thousands of dollars.

[1] After year 5, $21.79 remains to be recovered. This is 58% of the net cash flow for year 6.
[2] Assumes an 8.5% cost of capital.
[3] The value of the project at 8.5% is $269.52. Since the initial investment is $235.00, the profitability index is 1.15.

The internal rate of return is 11.8%. This is the rate that causes the present value of the ten net annual cash flows to exactly equal the initial investment of $235,000.

The net present value calculation for a project must assume a minimum required rate of return. As discussed in Chapter 3, net present value calculations require a minimum required rate of return. In this case, that rate is assumed to be 8.5%. The net present value is the difference between the value of the project, that is, the value of all the future cash flows, less the initial investment. The net present value of this expansion project is $34,520. Since the net present value is greater than zero, the project should be accepted. It represents an increase in shareholder value of $34,520 because its value exceeds its cost by this amount.

Notice that the internal rate of return exceeds the cost of capital and that the net present value is positive. The internal rate of return is that rate which causes the present value of the future cash flows to exactly equal the initial investment, resulting in a net present value of zero. Whenever the required return is less than the internal rate of return, the present value of the future cash flows will exceed the initial investment, resulting in a positive net present value. In the case of independent projects, this observation will always be true. Chapter 5 includes a discussion of conflicting results for mutually exclusive projects when net present value and internal rate of return result in different rankings.

The profitability index is 1.15. This means that the value of the project is 115% of the cost of the project. Notice that profitability index is a ratio of the same two elements that are used to compute net present value – the present value of the future cash flows and the initial investment. Net present value is the difference between these two elements. Profitability index is a ratio of the same two elements. Whenever the net present value is positive, the profitability index will be greater than one. Conversely, whenever the net present value is negative, the profitability index will be less than one.

Assuming that management is willing to take on projects whose payback period exceeds five years, this expansion project should be accepted based on these results. Note, however, that the results are sensitive to the estimation of future cash flows and the identification of the appropriate discount rate.

4

REPLACEMENT PROJECT EXAMPLE

When there is an existing project or technology in place, the capital budgeting decision becomes a replacement decision. The considerations that must be made are whether the existing technology should be abandoned and, at the same time, the new technology adopted. The process is once again to identify incremental cash flows – those that would be lost by abandoning the current project and those that would be gained by accepting the new project.

FIGURE 4.9

Replacement Project: Labor-saving Technology

New equipment:

Cost ($)	1,000
Useful life (years)	8
Anticipated salvage value ($)	100
Depreciation method	MACRS
Class life (years)	5
Annual cost savings ($)	250
Tax rate (%)	34

Old equipment:

Book value ($)	200
Current market value ($)	85
Remaining useful life (years)	8
Anticipated salvage value ($)	8
Depreciation method	straight line
Annual depreciation ($)	24

Note: Dollar amounts are in thousands.

Figure 4.9 sets out the details of a potential, labor-saving project, involving some sort of technological advance that permits cost savings in the production process. If this project is undertaken, the product mix of the firm will not change, as was true with the expansion project example. Instead, the project will reduce costs and boost profits.

Cost of the equipment is $1 million and it has a useful life of eight years. At the end of that eight-year life, the anticipated salvage value is $100,000. This equipment will also be depreciated using MACRS. The class life that applies here is five years because it is a computer application. If the project is accepted, the annual pre-tax cost savings will be $250,000 over the entire eight years of the project's useful life. Again, the tax rate that applies is 34%.

The equipment that is currently being used to serve the same function has a book value of $200,000. Because of technological advances, the current market value is considerably less – $85,000. Despite the fact that the current market value is relatively low compared to either the book value of the old equipment or the cost of the new equipment, the technology itself is serviceable and could continue to support the functions of the firm for another eight years. Thus, the remaining useful life of the existing equipment is eight years. The anticipated salvage value is a relatively modest $8,000. The equipment is being depreciated using straight-line method over the remaining eight years. Since the book value is $200,000 and anticipated salvage value is $8,000, the depreciable base that remains is $192,000, and this is being depreciated at the rate of $24,000 per year.

FIGURE 4.10

Replacement Project: Depreciation Schedule

Year	Depreciation Rate	Depreciation Amount (000s)
1	0.2000	200.0
2	0.3200	320.0
3	0.1920	192.0
4	0.1152	115.2
5	0.1152	115.2
6	0.0576	57.6

Figure 4.10 contains the depreciation amounts for this replacement project according to the five-year MACRS schedule. The first years are computed using the double-declining method with half-year convention, then switching to straight line in year 4. The sum of the rates for individual years is 1 and the depreciation amounts sum to exactly $1 million. When the planned depreciation is complete (at the end of year 6), the book value of this project will be zero.

Net Annual Cash Flows – Replacement Project

Figure 4.11 identifies the relevant cash flows for this project. At time zero, the cost of the new equipment is $1 million. That will be at least partially offset by the proceeds of $124,100 that are associated with selling the old equipment. This brings the negative cash flow at the time of acquisition (year 0) to a negative $875,900.

The annual cost savings over the life of the new equipment will amount to $165,000 on an after-tax basis. This amount is determined by multiplying the gross savings of $250,000 by the quantity $(1 - 0.34)$.

The depreciation tax shield associated with the new equipment is computed by multiplying the tax rate by the amount of depreciation per year that is allocated to the project. Since the depreciation amount varies from year to year, the depreciation tax shield also varies from year to year. However, the last tax shield associated with the new equipment occurs in year 6. With respect to the existing equipment, a level depreciation tax shield of $8,160 will be forgone or lost each year from year 1 through year 8. The difference between the depreciation tax shield associated with the new equipment and the forgone tax shield that is associated with the existing equipment is the *incremental depreciation tax shield*.

The sale of the projected equipment will occur in year 8, the end of its useful life. At that time, the book value of the equipment will be zero and any proceeds received will be fully taxable. On an after-tax basis, the net proceeds to the firm of selling this equipment at the end of its anticipated useful life is $66,000.

FIGURE 4.11

Replacement Project: Net Annual Cash Flows*

Year	0	1	2	3	4	5	6	7	8
Cost of new	(1,000.0)								
Cost savings[1]		165	165	165	165	165	165	165	165
DTS_N[2]		68	108.8	65.28	39.168	39.168	19.584		
Foregone DTS_E[2]		(8.16)	(8.16)	(8.16)	(8.16)	(8.16)	(8.16)	(8.16)	(8.16)
SV_N[3]									66
Foregone SV_E[4]									(8)
Sale of existing[5]	124.1								
	(875.9)	224.84	265.64	222.12	196.008	196.008	176.424	156.84	214.84

*In thousands of dollars.

[1] $CS(1 - t) = 250(1 - 0.34) = 165$

[2] $DTS_t = Dep(t) = Dep(0.34)$

[3] $SV = SV_N + (BV_N - SV_N)(t) = 100 + (0 - 100)(0.34) = 100(1 - 0.34) = 66$

[4] $SV = SV_E + (BV_E - SV_E)(t) = 8 + (8 - 8)(0.34)$

[5] $Sale = MV_E + (BV_E - MV_E)(t) = 85 + (200 - 85)(0.34) = 85 + 39.1 = 124.1$

The equipment that is currently being used will not be sold at the end of year 8. This is a cash flow that the firm forgoes if the decision is made to abandon the current equipment in year 0. The forgone salvage value of the existing equipment partially offsets the salvage value of the new equipment. Since the existing equipment is being depreciated to an $8,000 salvage value, the book value at the end of eight years will also be $8,000. If it is sold for $8,000 there will be neither a taxable gain or a tax-deductible loss. The full $8,000 proceeds would have been received by the firm without any tax impact whatsoever. The loss of this $8,000 must be reflected. The *incremental salvage value* is the after-tax difference between the anticipated salvage value of the proposed equipment and the forgone salvage value of the existing equipment – $58,000.

The last cash flow to be considered is the sale of the existing equipment. The sale of any capital asset may have tax implications. In this case, the book value of the equipment is $200,000 but its current market value is only $85,000. Thus, there will be a $115,000 loss that can be recorded at the time of acquisition. This loss can be used to offset other gains that the firm may realize and will generate a $39,100 tax benefit.[3] Adding the tax benefit to the gross proceeds of $85,000 yields a positive cash flow of $124,100. When this amount is netted against the cost of the new equipment, the net cash flow at the time of acquisition to a negative $875,900.

The positive cash flows that are the result of these components range from $156,840 in year 7 to $265,640 in year 2. These cash flows are the net annual amounts that will form the basis of a cash flow analysis and application of the capital budgeting techniques introduced in Chapter 3.

---

[3] At 34%, the tax benefit to be realized for a $115,000 write-off is $39,100.

Cash Flow Analysis – Replacement Project

Figure 4.12 is an analysis of the replacement project cash flows. The payback period is shown as 3.48 years or just under four years.

4

FIGURE 4.12

Replacement Project: Cash Flow Analysis*

Payback period (years)	3.8[1]
Internal rate of return (%)	17.97
Net present value[2] ($)	311.3
Profitability index	1.36[3]

*In thousands of dollars.

[1] After year 3, $163.30 remains to be recovered. This is 83% of the net cash flows for year 4.
[2] Assumes an 8.5% cost of capital.
[3] The value of the project at 8.5% is $1,187.16. Since the initial investment is $875.9, the profitability index is 1.36.

The internal rate of return is a relatively high 17.97%. If an 8.5% minimum required rate of return is assumed, this would be accepted. At the same time, the reinvestment assumptions that are incorporated into the internal rate of return must be considered. If a reinvestment rate of 18% is unrealistic, the firm should analyze the cash flows in Figure 4.11 by assigning a more realistic reinvestment rate, computing the terminal value, and then computing the expected return on this basis. See Chapter 3 for a discussion of reinvestment assumptions associated with internal rate of return.

The net present value is $311,300 assuming an 8.5% cost of capital. If this project is accepted, shareholder wealth will increase by this amount.

The profitability index is again consistent with the net present value findings. The profitability index is 1.36 which means that every dollar of net investment returns a value of $1.36. Again when the net present value is positive, the profitability index will be greater than one. Also, when the internal rate of return exceeds the cost of capital, the net present value will be positive (and the profitability index will be greater than one).

Given that management is willing to accept projects with a payback period of four years or less, this project is acceptable. It earns a rate of return that is higher than the minimum and it increases shareholder wealth. Of course, any changes in the assumptions with respect to cash flow, salvage value, or appropriate rate of return, will modify the results accordingly.

SUMMARY

The cash flows that are necessary to apply the concepts of payback period, internal rate of return, net present value, and profitability index are typically composed of several components. These components include:

- cost
- installation
- working capital changes
- revenue changes
- cost savings
- increased expense
- depreciation tax shield
- cash flows from salvage values
- cash flows from sale of existing equipment, in the case of a replacement project.

In each case, it is cash flows, not income, that must be considered. Also, all cash flows must be stated on an after-tax basis. Converting before-tax cash flows to after-tax cash flows will require adjustments that depend on:

- whether or not the item is a capital asset;
- whether or not the item is a cash or noncash item.

For each relevant year of the analysis, net annual cash flows must be determined. Once this has been achieved, the capital budgeting techniques may be applied with the appropriate decision rules.

4

CHAPTER 5

SPECIAL SITUATIONS

INTRODUCTION

The concepts and tools that are described in Chapters 1–4 are the fundamental approaches to capital budgeting decisions. However, certain special considerations are necessary when analyzing mutually exclusive projects. These situations are:

■ conflicting rankings
■ projects of different scale or required investment
■ projects with unequal lives.

In addition, there are modifications of the net present value approach that should be used when inflation adjustments are required.

CONFLICTING RANKINGS OF MUTUALLY EXCLUSIVE PROJECTS

In all cases, net present value and internal rate of return will not yield consistent rankings when mutually exclusive projects must be considered. Figure 5.1 provides an example of such a situation. Projects A and B both require an initial investment of $1,000. Both have an expected

FIGURE 5.1						
Mutually Exclusive Projects						
Year	0	1	2	3	4	5
Project A	(1,000)	100	800	450	25	100
Project B	(1,000)	0	20	270	735	800
		IRR (%)		NPV ($)*		
Project A		17.485		169.33		
Project B		15.291		218.14		
*Assumes a 10% cost of capital.						

93

useful life of five years. The net annual cash flows of each project are given in Figure 5.1.

Based on these cash flows, the internal rate of return (IRR) of Project A is 17.485% while that of project B is 15.291%.[1] If IRR is used as a decision criterion, the decision should be to accept Project A because it has the higher IRR. At the same time, if a 10% cost of capital is assumed, the net present value (NPV) approach yields a ranking that is exactly the opposite. At 10%, Project A has a net present value of $169.33 while Project B's NPV is $218.14.[2] Since the net present value of Project B is higher than that of Project A, project B has a higher ranking than Project A. In such situations, NPV should be considered the primary decision-making tool because NPV measures the increase in shareholder wealth that will be realized if a project is accepted. The cost of capital is assumed to be the rate of return that is available on investors' next best alternative investment.

NPV versus IRR

The first insight into understanding these conflicting rankings is to realize that IRR is a unique rate of return that will not change as long as the cash flows are assumed to be at the stated levels. IRR is the rate of return that will cause the present value of specific cash flows to equal a specific initial investment. On the other hand, NPV is the present value of future flows at an objectively determined rate of return. To the extent that the discount rate changes, the net present value will also change.

---

[1] The internal rate of return is that rate which causes the present value of cash flows during years 1 through 5 to exactly equal the amount of the initial investment. See Chapter 3 for a discussion of the internal rate of return.

[2] Net present value is the difference between the present value of the future cash flows, discounted at 10%, and the initial investment that is required. See Chapter 3 for a discussion of net present value.

FIGURE 5.2

Mutually Exclusive Projects: Net Present Value

Discount Rate (%)	Net Present Value	
	Project A ($)	Project B ($)
0	475.0	825.0
5	308.5	482.9
10	169.3	218.1
15	51.8	10.6
20	−48.5	−153.9
25	−134.6	−285.8
30	−209.2	−392.5
35	−274.2	−479.6
40	−331.3	−551.3
45	−381.7	−610.8
50	−426.3	−660.6

5

Figure 5.2 shows the impact on net present value for both Projects A and B when the discount rate changes. Notice that at a discount rate of 0%, the net present value of each project is simply the difference between:

- summation of the future cash flows; and
- initial investment.

At a zero discount rate, the net present value of both of these projects is maximized. This is a general rule. When the discount rate is 0%, the present value of future cash flows is unaffected by time and, thus, the time value of money has no impact.

As the discount rate increases, however, the present value of the future cash flows decreases. At the same time, the initial investment remains unaffected by the time value of money because no time elapses between:

- timing of the initial investment; and
- the point of valuation of the initial investment.

Both are at time zero (see Appendix A for time value of money concepts). The combination of declining present values of future cash flows with a constant initial investment causes net present value to decline as the discount rate increases. This is illustrated in Figure 5.2. The net present value of Project A at a 0% rate of return is $475. NPV$_A$ drops consistently to a negative $426.30 at 50%. This means that the present value of the future cash flows is $573.70, while the initial investment is $1,000 which yields a negative net present value of $426.30.

$$NPV_A = 573.70 - 1,000 = -426.30 \qquad (1)$$

The same general pattern is identified for Project B. At a 0% rate of return, the net present value of the project is $825. As the discount rate increases, net present value declines. The decreases are more accelerated for Project B than for Project A, however. At a 50% discount rate the net present value of Project B is negative $660.60. This means that at a 50% discount rate, the present value of the future cash flows of Project B is $339.40 while its initial investment is $1,000.

$$NPV_B = 339.40 - 1,000 = -660.60 \qquad (2)$$

From a 0% discount rate to a 50% discount rate, the rankings of the two projects change. At a 0% rate, Project B is preferable to Project A. At a 50% discount rate neither project is acceptable but Project A results in a smaller loss of value than Project B. Thus, the rankings shift as the discount rate increased.

Net Present Value Profile

The *net present value profiles* of these two projects are useful in analyzing this reversal of rankings. Figure 5.3 outlines the characteristics of a net present value profile. Essentially, the net present value profile, or NPV profile, is a graphic representation of the sensitivity of a project's NPV to the discount rate used.

5

FIGURE 5.3

Net Present Value Profile

Graphic representation of sensitivity of project NPV to discount rate:

When $k = 0$, NPV is simple summation of all cash flows.

When $k = $ IRR, NPV equals 0.

When $k < $ IRR, NPV is positive.

When $k > $ IRR, NPV is negative.

The important features of the NPV profile are as follows.

- The NPV profile plots discount rate on the x-axis and NPV on the y-axis.
- When the discount rate is 0, NPV is the summation of future cash flows less the initial investment. This is true because, when *k is zero*, the process of dividing each cash flow by $(1 + k)^n$ (to find present value) is equivalent to dividing each cash flow by 1. The simple summation of futures cash flows less initial investment is the y-intercept of the NPV profile.
- The NPV profile declines as the discount rate increases from zero, that is, the NPV profile has a negative slope. As k increases, the quantity $(1 + k)^n$ increases and the present value declines.

- When the discount rates equals IRR of a project, the NPV is zero. This can be seen by recalling that NPV is the difference between the present value of future cash flows and the initial investment. IRR is the rate that causes the present value of future cash flows to exactly equal the initial investment. Thus, when the discount rate equals IRR, the present value of future cash flows equals the initial investment, that is, NPV is zero. IRR is the x-intercept of the NPV profile.

- When the discount rate is less than IRR, net present value is positive. At a rate lower than IRR, the present value of future cash flows is greater than the initial investment.

- When the discount rate is greater than IRR, NPV is negative. At a rate higher than IRR, the present value of future cash flows is less than the initial investment.

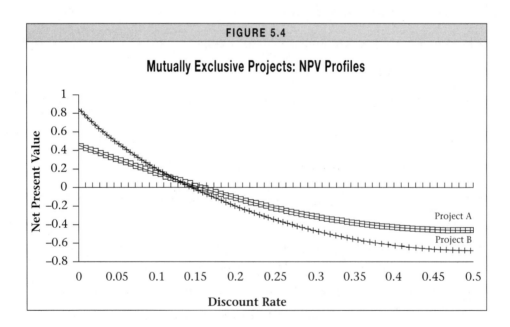

FIGURE 5.4

Mutually Exclusive Projects: NPV Profiles

Figure 5.4 illustrates the NPV profiles for Projects A and B (described in Figure 5.1). Notice that the y-intercept is intersected by Project A at $475 and by Project B at $825. This is consistent with the data in Figure 5.2. These amounts are the NPVs of the respective projects when the discount rate is zero and represent the maximum net present values for each project. As the discount rate increases from 0, the NPVs of both projects decline. However, the NPV of Project B declines faster. At some rate of return that is less than each project's IRR, the NPV profiles cross. Both NPVs remain positive for all discount rates that are less than their respective IRRs. For rates higher than each project's IRR, the NPV profile of each is negative.

The discount rate at which both NPVs are equal is the *crossover rate*, or k^*. At k^*, the net present values of both projects are equal. In order to find this rate, the two NPVs are set equal and the equation is solved for k. NPV_A (at some unknown k) equals NPV_B (at the same unknown k), and the unknown discount rate equals k^*, as shown below.

$$\frac{100}{(1+k^*)} + \frac{800}{(1+k^*)^2} + \frac{450}{(1+k^*)^3} + \frac{25}{(1+k^*)^4} + \frac{100}{(1+k^*)^5} - 1{,}000 =$$

$$\frac{0}{(1+k^*)} + \frac{20}{(1+k^*)^2} + \frac{270}{(1+k^*)^3} + \frac{735}{(1+k^*)^4} + \frac{800}{(1+k^*)^5} - 1{,}000 \tag{3}$$

Notice that the left-hand side of equation 3 is the NPV of Project A and the right-hand side of equation 3 is the NPV of Project B. Since the initial investment is the same for both projects, adding $1,000 to both sides leaves the present value of future cash flows discounted at the crossover rate of k^*. Subtracting all the terms on the right-hand side from both sides of the equation will leave zero on the right-hand side and the difference between the terms on the left-hand side as follows.

$$\frac{100}{(1+k^*)} + \frac{780}{(1+k^*)^2} + \frac{180}{(1+k^*)^3} - \frac{710}{(1+k^*)^4} - \frac{700}{(1+k^*)^5} = 0 \tag{4}$$

Equation 4 is equivalent to a five-year project with initial investment of zero and future cash flows of $100, $780, $180, –$710, and –$700. The rate of return (IRR) that will cause the present value of these future cash flows to equal zero (as stipulated in equation 4) is 12.505%, the crossover rate for Projects A and B. Using 12.505% to compute net present values, the NPV of each project is $108.02.

It is now clear that Project B will be preferable to Project A at all discount rates less than 12.505%. Project A will be preferable to Project B only for rates in excess of 12.505% and less than or equal to 17.485%. At 17.485%, the IRR of Project A, Project A's net present value is zero. For any rates in excess of 17.485% the net present values of Project A and Project B are negative, and neither project should be accepted.

The NPV profile in this case illustrates the sensitivity of the decision to discount rate. It also illustrates the steeper slope of the NPV profile of Project B. Examining the actual cash flows in Figure 5.1 reveals the reason for the steeper slope of the NPV profile of Project B. Notice that Project B returns almost nothing in years 1 and 2. The bulk of its cash flows occur in years 4 and 5. These cash flows are more sensitive to the effect of changing discount rate because they are received further in the future. Project A cash flows are greater in the earlier years of the project and are less sensitive to changes in interest rate than Project B.

Thus, the NPV profile helps to resolve conflicting rankings for mutually exclusive projects. It also shows that projects with significantly different patterns of future cash flow will have different sensitivities to changes in discount rate.

COMPARING PROJECTS WITH DIFFERENT REQUIRED INVESTMENTS

Another difference that can arise among mutually exclusive projects is the general level of required investment. Figure 5.5 illustrates two projects of this kind. Project A requires a $1,000 investment while Project B requires only a $200 investment. When the two projects are analyzed it is found that the IRR of Project A is 20.7%, while the IRR of Project B is 36.3%. On the other hand, the NPV of Project A is $291.20, while that of Project B is $140.90. Comparing the two projects' profitability indexes, the PI of Project A is 1.29 times while the PI of Project B is 1.70 times.

FIGURE 5.5

Projects of Different Scale

	0	1	2	3	4	5
Project A	(1,000)	250	400	350	575	125
Project B	(200)	50	180	70	115	25
Project A-B	(800)	200	220	280	460	100

	IRR (%)	NPV ($)*	PI*
Project A	20.7	291.2	1.29
Project B	36.3	140.9	1.70
Project A-B	16.9	150.3	1.19

* Assumes a 10% cost of capital.

The rankings for these two projects conflict. Using the IRR decision criterion, Project B is preferable to Project A. According to NPV, Project A is preferable to Project B. According to PI, Project B is preferable to Project A.

Generally, more consideration should be given to the NPV ranking in arriving at the correct decision in these cases. The NPV calculations show that shareholder wealth would be increased by $291.20 if Project A is accepted, despite the fact that it does have a lower profitability index than Project B. The investment that is required for Project A is five times the investment required for Project B. Each dollar invested in Project B returns $1.70 in (the present value of) future cash flows. On the other hand, Project A returns $1.29 for each dollar invested.

The difference between the two projects in terms of their initial investment and their future cash flows can be analyzed by examining the difference between them. This third project, A-B, requires an $800 initial investment and returns cash flows in each of the next five years of $200, $220, $280, $460, and $100. Project A-B has an IRR of 16.9% and an NPV of $150.30. Hence Project A-B is an acceptable project because it has a rate of return that is higher than the 10% cost of capital, and a positive NPV of $150.30.

Assuming for a moment that the choices are either Project B or Project A-B, Project A-B has a higher NPV than Project B and is thus more advisable. Furthermore, if $200 were invested in Project B and the $600 difference invested in the firm's next best investment alternative (earning the 10% cost of capital), the same amount of investment would be required for Project B as for Project A-B. Since the $600 increment would be invested at 10%, the NPV would be 0 and the profitability index would be 1. The weighted average profitability index of this combination is 1.175 [(2/8)(1.70) + (6/8)(1)], lower than the profitability index of Project A-B of 1.19. Again, Project A-B is preferable to Project B.

If it were possible to accept *both* Project A-B and Project B, shareholders would be that much better off since both have a positive NPV. But Project A-B and Project B are simply Project A. Thus, Project A dominates in this situation of projects with different scale.

When there are projects of different scale, it is important to analyze the incremental difference between the two. If the incremental difference is acceptable and the smaller project is acceptable, then the larger project generally should be accepted.

COMPARING PROJECTS WITH UNEQUAL LIVES

Another important special situation in capital budgeting is the comparison of projects with unequal lives. Figure 5.6 illustrates two new mutually exclusive projects, A and B, with the same initial required investment
but substantially different useful lives. Project A has a six-year useful life
and Project B a two-year life. When the conventional measures of
IRR, NPV, and PI are considered, IRR suggests that Project B should be
accepted because its IRR is 31.0% versus 23.9% for Project A. On the other
hand, NPV suggests that Project A should be accepted because the NPV of
A ($27.43) is $6.07 higher than the NPV of Project B ($21.36). The PIs of
the two projects are virtually the same – 1.27 for Project A and 1.21 for
Project B. Each dollar of investment in Project A returns $1.27 in (present
value of) future cash flows. Each dollar invested in Project B returns $1.21.

FIGURE 5.6

Projects with Unequal Lives

	0	1	2	3	4	5	6
Project A	(100)	35	15	42	37	22	60
Project B	(100)	70	80				

	IRR (%)	NPV($)*	PI*
Project A	23.9	27.43	1.27
Project B	31.0	21.36	1.21

* Assumes a 15% cost of capital.

The problem with analyzing these two projects is that there are no cash
flows associated with Project B in years 3, 4, 5, and 6. The measures that
may be used to adjust for this difference in cash flow stream, that is, difference in expected life, are:

- equivalent annual annuity
- replication.

Equivalent Annual Annuity Approach

Net present value is the total of the present values of all cash flows associated with a project. If NPV is considered the present value of an annuity, there is some annuity over the useful life that is equivalent to this present value.[3] If these *equivalent annual annuities* (EAAs) are computed for the projects in Figure 5.6, Project B is preferable to Project A.

FIGURE 5.7

Projects with Unequal Lives: Equivalent Annual Annuity

Formula	$NPV = EAA\ (PVIFA_{k,n})$

Project A

$$27.43 = EAA\ (PVIFA_{0.15,6})$$
$$27.43 = EAA\ (3.7845)$$
$$EAA = 27.43/3.7845$$
$$= 7.25$$

Project B

$$21.36 = EAA\ (PVIFA_{0.15,2})$$
$$21.36 = EAA\ (1.6257)$$
$$EAA = 21.36/1.6257$$
$$= 13.14$$

To see this, recall that the net present value of Project A is $27.43, while that of Project B is $21.36. If both of these amounts are considered to be the present values of annuities at a 15% cost of capital, then the equivalent in terms of annual payments may be found. The approach is to find the equal

---

[3] Appendix A discusses time value of money concepts and Appendix B contains present value and future value factors.

annual payment that will cause the present value of the payments for the applicable period of time to exactly equal the net present value.

$$NPV = EAA(PVIFA_{k,n}) \tag{5}$$

Figure 5.7 shows the calculation of EAAs for Project A and Project B. Since Project A is a six-year project, the appropriate annuity factor is for the combination of 15% and six years. This factor is 3.7845 which, when substituted into the present value of annuity formula, implies an EAA of $7.25 – the equivalent of an annuity in this amount for each of the six years.

In the case of Project B, the appropriate annuity factor is for the combination of 15% and two years. Since that factor is 1.6257 and the net present value of Project A the project is $21.36, the EAA is $13.14 – the equivalent of an annuity in this amount for each of the two years.

The approach of equivalent annual annuity, EAA, suggests that Project B is preferable. Despite the fact that the net present value of B is less than the net present value of A, the shorter life of Project B effectively means that more is received for each of the two years of the life of the project. This approach takes into account the useful life of the projects and measures the effective cash flows that will be received on average for each of the years of useful life of the project.

Replication Approach

Another way to analyze these two projects is to compensate directly for the shorter life of Project B. This can be accomplished by assuming *replication* of Project B so that it will have a total useful life which equals the useful life of Project A. Since Project A has a six-year useful life and Project B only a two-year life, it is necessary to replicate Project B three times so that the combined useful life of that project, when replicated, is also six years.

FIGURE 5.8

Projects with Unequal Lives: Replication

	0	1	2	3	4	5	6
Project A							
Cash flows	(100)	35	15	42	37	22	60
NPV	27.43						
Project B							
Cash flows							
1st replication	(100)	70	80				
2nd replication			(100)	70	80		
3rd replication					(100)	70	80
NPV	21.36		21.36		21.36		

Totals

$$\text{NPV}_A = \underline{27.43}$$
$$\text{NPV}_B = \overline{21.36} + 21.36/(1.15)^2 + 21.36/(1.15)^4$$
$$= 21.36 + 16.15 + 12.21$$
$$= \underline{49.72}$$

Figure 5.8 shows how this may be done. Project cash flows and NPVs are shown for the relevant replications. In the case of Project A, NPV of $27.43 at time zero reflects the value of all cash flows for year 0 through year 6.

For Project B, the first step is to identify the first replication of the project which provides a net present value of $21.36 as of year 0. If the project is repeated, the next replication will require a reinvestment of $100 immediately after the last cash flow for the first replication at the end of year 2. Thus, a $100 investment is made once again, immediately after the $80 payment for that period. In the second replication, the cash flows of $70 and $80 occur in years 3 and 4, respectively. This produces a net present value for the second replication of $21.36 as of year 2, the year of investment for the second replication. The third replication requires an investment of $100 immediately after the $80 payment associated with replication 2 – year 4. If the $100 of required investment is made at that time, then the two future cash flows of $70 and $80 occur in years 5 and 6, respectively. This means that the net present value of the third replication is valued at $21.36 as of year 4.

The bottom of Figure 5.8 shows the total net present values, given all relevant replications. Of course, for Project A, the net present value is simply the $27.43 associated with the single replication of that project. For Project B, the $21.36 net present value of replication 1 is added to the present values of replications 2 ($16.15) and 3 ($12.21) to arrive at a total net present value for Project B of $49.72 – which exceeds the $27.43 NPV of Project A. Thus, once again, it is shown that Project B is preferable to Project A when compensation is made for the difference in useful lives.

In essence, the replication approach forces mutually exclusive projects to be considered for the same number of years despite the fact that they have unequal lives. In this case, replication was required only for Project B because the useful life of Project B was evenly divisible into the useful life of Project A. When the useful life of one project is not a whole-number multiple of the useful life of the other, it may be necessary to replicate both projects. For example, if one project has a useful life of four years and the second project has a useful life of three years, it will be necessary to replicate the first project three times and the second project four times, so that a common denominator of 12 years of useful life can be achieved. Whatever the combination, the important point to remember is that replication compensates for mutually exclusive projects that have unequal lives.

ADJUSTING FOR INFLATION

It may also be desirable to adjust cash flows for the effects of *inflation*. Inflation is the loss of the purchasing power of money, that is, an increase in prices that is not associated with any increase in quality or quantity of goods. Inflation should be analyzed as part of the nominal required rate of return, where the nominal rate is the rate which is quoted or stated in contractual terms. The excess of the nominal rate of return over inflation is the real rate of return.

The Fisher Effect

In other words, the real rate, k^*, and the nominal rate, k_{nom}, are connected by the rate of inflation.[4] The nominal rate includes both the real rate and the inflation rate. This is referred to as the *Fisher Effect* and is illustrated in Figure 5.9. Notice that the nominal rate includes the real rate of return, the inflation rate, and a cross-product of the two rates.

FIGURE 5.9

Adjusting for Inflation: Fisher Effect

$$(1 + k_{nom}) = (1 + k^*)(1 + I)$$
$$1 + k_{nom} = 1 + k^* + I + k^*I$$
$$k_{nom} = k^* + I + k^*I$$

where k_{nom} = nominal rate
k^* = real rate
I = inflation rate

---

[4] In this case, k^* is simply notation for the real rate of return and should not be confused with the crossover rate in connection with the NPV profile.

The rationale for this relationship can be explained by a simple example. Suppose that an investor wishes to invest sufficient funds today to make a purchase one year from today. The purchase price of the item in question is $110. If the investor, in the absence of inflation, invests $100 today at a 10% rate of return, that investor will achieve the goal of accumulating the necessary purchase price of $110.

However, if inflation is 5%, the investor must earn more than 10% on the $100 investment because the purchase price of the product will increase. It is not sufficient to increase the rate of return on the $100 investment by 5 percentage points. This can be seen by calculating the actual price of the $110 item in one year, assuming 5% inflation.

$$P_1 = 110(1.05) = 115.50 \qquad (6)$$

At the end of one year, the price of the item will have grown from $110 to $115.50. The investor will not reach the stated goal of $115.50 at the rate of return on investment of 15% (10% real return + 5% inflation). Instead, it is necessary for the rate of return on investment also to grow by 5% [(0.05)(0.10)], that is, the product of k^* and I, must be added. In this case, the investor must earn 15.5%.

FIGURE 5.10

Adjusting for Inflation: Solving for the Real Rate of Return

$$(1 + k_{nom}) = (1 + k^*)(1 + I)$$
$$(1 + k^*) = (1 + k_{nom})/(1 + I)$$
$$k^* = (1 + k_{nom})/(1 + I) - 1$$

Substituting,

$$k^* = (1.15)/(1.05) - 1$$
$$= 0.0952$$

In Figure 5.10, the objective was to find the nominal rate of return that would enable an investor to achieve a stated goal. In adjusting cash flows of capital projects for inflation, the Fisher Effect can be used to arrive at the real rate of return that is implied by market rates. This amounts to solving the Fisher Effect equation for k^*, as illustrated in Figure 5.10. Using the earlier example of a project with a 15% rate of return and assuming a 5% inflation rate, the real rate of return is 9.52%.

Thus, there are two ways to adjust for inflation. The first is to assume that the project cash flows are real cash flows, i.e., they have not been adjusted for inflation. These cash flows are then discounted using the real rate of return.

The second method is to adjust the cash flows themselves for inflation and then to discount these cash flows by the nominal rate of return (which includes an adjustment for inflation).

FIGURE 5.11

Adjusting for Inflation: Cash Flows

	0	1	2	3	4	5	6
Project A							
Real cash flows:							
Cost	(100)						
Revenue		29.33	3.67	30.67	31.33	22.00	60.00
DTS		5.67	11.33	11.33	5.67	–	–
	(100)	35.00	15.00	42.00	37.00	22.00	60.00
Inflation-adjusted cash flows:							
Cost	(100)						
Revenue[1]		30.80	4.05	35.50	38.08	28.08	80.41
DTS		5.67	11.33	11.33	5.67	–	–
	(100)	36.47	15.38	46.83	43.75	28.08	80.41

[1] After-tax revenues are expected to increase at the rate of 5%.

Adjusting Cash Flows

Figure 5.11 uses Project A, introduced in Figure 5.6. In this case, the cash flows of the project are separated into two components. The first component is revenue that will be realized in each year over the life of the project. The second is a depreciation tax shield that will be realized during years 1–4 assuming a three-year useful life and a half-year convention.[5] When these component cash flows are added together, the net annual cash flows are the same as those shown in Figure 5.6 and should be considered the real cash flows of the project. This means that the net annual cash flows will be discounted using the real rate of return of 9.52% (computed in Figure 5.10).

If these cash flows are adjusted for inflation, assuming a 5% rate of inflation, the result is shown in the bottom portion of Figure 5.11. Notice that the depreciation tax shield does not increase with inflation because the depreciation tax shield is computed based on the historical cost of the initial investment. On the other hand, revenues are realized each year and increase with inflation. For year 1, the adjustment for inflation is to multiply the real revenue of $29.33 by 1.05 which is 1 plus the inflation rate. This produces an inflation-adjusted cash flow in year 1 of $30.80. The adjustment for year 2 is to multiply the real cash flow of $3.67 by $(1.05)^2$ since two years will have elapsed at 5% inflation in each year. This results in a year 2 cash flow of $4.05.

Each cash flow is adjusted for inflation in a similar fashion, taking into account the number of years that will elapse between time zero and the year of cash receipt. The basic approach is to compound at the rate of inflation for the appropriate number of periods that elapse between time

---

[5] The depreciable base of Project A is $100. When this base is depreciated over a three-year life using straight-line depreciation, the half-year convention, and a tax rate of 34%, the write-off in the first year is $33.33 but the half-year convention reduces this to $16.67. Multiplying $16.67 by the tax rate of 34% produces a depreciation tax shield of $5.67. The write-off in year 2 is $33.33. When this is multiplied by the 34% tax rate, the depreciation tax shield is $11.33. The remaining depreciation tax shields for years 3 and 4 are computed in a similar manner. See Chapter 4 for a discussion of depreciation methods.

zero and the point of actual cash flow. (See Appendix A for an explanation of the future value of a single amount.) Once the revenues have been adjusted for inflation and added to the depreciation tax shield (not adjusted for inflation), the net cash flows for Project A in years 1–6 are $36.47, $15.38, $46.83, $43.75, $28.08, and $80.41, respectively.

Net Present Value

Figure 5.12 shows the computation of net present value using both methods of adjusting for inflation. In the first case, real cash flows are discounted by 9.52%, the real rate of return. This produces a net present value of $50.88. This is the conventional cash-flow stream discounted by a real rate of return, which, in turn, is derived from the market rate of return and inflation expectations.

The bottom portion of Figure 5.12 is the alternative method of adjust-

---

FIGURE 5.12

Adjusting for Inflation: NPV

Project A
Real cash flows:
$$NPV = 35/(1.0952) + 15/(1.0952)^2 + 42/(1.0952)^3 +$$
$$37/(1.0952)^4 + 22/(1.0952)^5 + 60/(1.0952)^6 - 100$$
$$= 31.9576 + 12.5056 + 31.9719 +$$
$$25.7175 + 13.9623 + 34.7689 - 100$$
$$= 50.88$$

Inflation-adjusted cash flows:
$$NPV = 36.47/(1.15) + 15.38/(1.15)^2 + 46.83/(1.15)^3 +$$
$$43.75/(1.15)^4 + 28.08/(1.15)^5 + 80.41/(1.15)^6 - 100$$
$$= 31.7130 + 11.6295 + 30.7915 +$$
$$25.0142 + 13.9607 + 34.7635 - 100$$
$$= 47.87$$

ing for inflation. In this case, the cash flows (adjusted for inflation) are discounted by the 15% nominal rate of return (which already includes an adjustment for anticipated inflation). The net present value is $47.87.

Notice that both inflation-adjusted net present values are higher than the conventional computation which was $27.43 (Figures 5.6 and 5.8). The reason for this result is that cash flows in the original calculation of NPV were not adjusted for inflation, but the discount rate of 15% included an inflation expectation. When these same cash flows are discounted at the implied real rate of return (a lower rate), a higher net present value results.[6] Likewise, when the discount rate is maintained at 15% and the cash flows themselves increase through inflation adjustments, the result is a higher net present value. This occurs because higher cash flows are discounted at the same discount rate, producing a higher net present value.

SUMMARY

The need for special considerations sometimes arises when making decisions with respect to capital projects. When projects are mutually exclusive, a ranking of projects by NPV may produce a different ordering of the projects than a ranking by IRR. In such cases, reference to the projects' NPV profile can be useful. Typically, NPV profiles will help to identify the range of discount rates over which one project will dominate the others.

Another situation that will sometimes produce conflicting rankings is the comparison of projects of different scale. These are projects that require significantly different initial investments. In such cases, it is often useful to analyze the differential cash flows of the two projects.

When projects have unequal lives, it is necessary to adjust for this difference. One adjustment is to determine an equivalent annual annuity,

---

[6] When a lower discount rate is used, all other things being equal, the present value will increase.

which establishes the effective annual payment that each project yields over its useful life. An alternative adjustment for unequal lives is to replicate the projects for the least-common-denominator number of years of useful life.

It is possible to adjust for inflation either by discounting projected cash flows (unadjusted for inflation) by the real rate of return, which is the market rate after adjustment for inflation. An alternative method is to adjust cash flows, as applicable, and then to discount these inflation-adjusted cash flows by the nominal rate of return.

In any of the methods discussed above, the approach is to apply a reasonable and consistent standard of treatment to the cash flows and to the discount rate. Factors that should be taken into consideration are relative magnitude of initial investment, timing of subsequent cash flows, the period of time over which future cash flows will be realized, and whether the cash flows have been appropriately adjusted for inflation.

CHAPTER 6

THE LEASING DECISION

INTRODUCTION

Leases are now an important source of financing for assets, from major asset acquisitions to items of office equipment. These transactions can range from $2,000 to $10 million. The type of equipment that can be leased is varied, including, but not limited to:

- agriculture and dairy equipment
- air compressors
- aircraft
- ATM machines
- automotive equipment – commercial
- automotive equipment – personal
- baling equipment (compactors)
- carpeting and tiles
- computer software
- computers and copiers
- construction equipment
- graphics equipment
- laundry equipment
- lighting, sound, and video systems
- machinery and machine tools
- medical equipment
- office furniture and equipment
- point-of-sale (POS) systems
- printing equipment
- shelving and cabinets.

Leasing has become an alternative means of financing. Some of the advantages that are often cited are:

- a minimal initial cash outlay permitting conservation of cash flow for other investment opportunities;

6

- lease payments that are fixed throughout the lease term to permit accurate budgeting of operating expenses;
- many lease payments that are deductible for income tax purposes;
- the ability to operate competitively with the latest technology and the flexibility of changing equipment to remain competitive.

The leasing decision is in addition to the capital budgeting decision. Once a project is considered acceptable according to established criteria, the decision is whether to *lease* or *purchase*.

TYPES OF LEASE

Leases can fulfill various functions for the firm. In some cases, equipment is leased on an extremely short-term basis. In other cases, the equipment is leased for considerably longer periods of time. There is a fundamental economic difference between short-term and long-term leases, with long-term leases representing a form of long-term financing. Figure 6.1 contains the basic lease classifications and highlights the differences.

Operating Leases

The first type is an *operating lease*, which should be used when the requirement for an asset is temporary in nature, for example the need for transportation during an out-of-town business trip. An automobile rental satisfies this temporary need. Because of the temporary nature of such needs, operating leases are necessarily short-term.

Furthermore, the lessee (equipment user) receives no rights of ownership under an operating lease. The lessor (owner of the equipment) retains all rights of ownership and responsibility for maintenance of the equipment. An operating lease does not appear on the balance sheet of the lessee. The leased asset remains on the balance sheet of the lessor. Accordingly, the lessor retains the right to depreciate the equipment, while the lessee is entitled to deduct the lease payment as an operating expense.

FIGURE 6.1

Types of Lease

Operating lease
- Temporary need
- Short-term
- Off-balance sheet
- Cancelable

Financial lease
- Long-term
- Off-balance sheet
- Non-cancelable

Capital lease
- Long-term
- On-balance sheet
- Non-cancelable

6

Financial Leases

On the other hand, a *financial lease* has characteristics that are more in common with long-term borrowing for the purpose of purchasing an asset. Effectively, a purchaser uses a financial lease to pay for a major asset. Unlike a long-term loan or other borrowing arrangement, however, the financial lease does not appear on the balance sheet of the lessee. Instead, lease payments are deducted as an operating expense for tax purposes. In a strictly financial lease, the lessee does not deduct depreciation for the asset being used. Nevertheless, as is true for long-term borrowing to finance an asset, the obligation under the lease may not be canceled.

The financial lease enjoyed increasing popularity prior to 1976 because it enabled lessees to avoid recording liabilities on the balance sheet. While the entire lease payment was deducted from income, lessees avoided recording the interest expense and depreciation expense that would have been recorded if the assets had been purchased using conventional debt financing.

Capital Leases

In 1976, the US Financial Accounting Standards Board (FASB) released Statement of Financial Accounting Standards No. 13, *Accounting for Leases.*[1] This statement attempted to equalize the treatment of all leases that were used primarily as financing vehicles by establishing standards for the *capital lease.* A capital lease is essentially a long-term lease that is recorded on the balance sheet of the lessee. Like the strictly financial lease, the capital lease is also non-cancelable. The difference is that the existence of a long-term liability (obligation to make the lease payments) and the associated long-term asset (right to use the asset) are recorded on the lessee's balance sheet.

DEFINING THE CAPITAL LEASE

SFAS No. 13 outlines the definition of a capital lease. It also stipulates the conditions under which a lease must be classified as a capital lease and

---

FIGURE 6.2

Capital Lease

- Transfers ownership to lessee before lease expiration.

- Entitles lessee to purchase asset for a bargain price at time of lease expiration.

- Lasts for at least 75% of the project's estimated economic life.

- Involves lease payments whose present value is at least 90% of the asset's value.

---

[1] The Financial Accounting Standards Board is a seven-member independent board, based in Norwalk, Connecticut, USA. This body sets accounting rules for certified public accountants and its Statements of Financial Accounting Standards are the basis for Generally Accepted Accounting Principles.

shown on the books of the lessee. If any one of four conditions are present, a lease must be treated as a capital lease.

Figure 6.2 outlines these conditions. The first is a *transfer of ownership* from the lessor to the lessee prior to expiration of the lease. This means that if the lessee becomes the legal owner (that is, obtains legal title to the asset) before the end of the lease, the lease must necessarily be accounted for as a capital lease.

The second condition is a *bargain purchase price*. If the lessee has the right to purchase the asset at the time of lease expiration for an amount that is substantially below market value, the lease is considered to be a tool for financing the purchase of the asset.

The term of the lease will also have some impact on whether or not it is considered a capital lease. If the term of the lease is *at least 75% of the anticipated useful life* of the asset, the lease will be accounted for as a capital lease.

The amount of the lease payments will have an impact. Should the present value of lease payments under the terms of the lease *exceed 90% of the value of the asset*, the lease will qualify as a capital lease.

Capital Lease Classification – Example

Figure 6.3 contains the details of a delivery truck that will be leased by the user of the truck. The estimated useful life of the truck is five years, but

FIGURE 6.3	
Long-term Lease: Delivery Truck	
Estimated economic life (years)	5
Term of lease (years)	4
Market value ($)	40,000
Annual lease payment ($)	10,522.85
Interest rate (%)	8
Residual value ($)	7,000

the term of the lease is only four years. If the user of the equipment were to buy the truck, the purchase price would be $40,000. But the manufacturer of the truck offers the use of the truck for four years with annual payments of $10,522.85. The payments in this case will be made at the end of each of the next four years (clearly very favorable terms). The appropriate interest rate to evaluate this lease arrangement is 8%, the cost of debt for the lessee in this case. At the end of the term of the lease, it is possible for the lessee to obtain ownership of the truck if a residual value of $7,000 is paid. These aspects of the lease are analyzed to determine whether the lease should be classified as a capital lease (on-balance-sheet) or as a non-capitalized financial lease (off-balance-sheet).

The four tests are analyzed in Figure 6.4. The first test is the transfer of ownership test. Recall that if the ownership of the equipment transfers to

---

FIGURE 6.4

Delivery Truck: Test for Lease Capitalization

Transfer of Ownership
Ownership does not transfer before lease expiration.

Bargain Purchase Price upon Expiration
Residual value of $7,000 is anticipated fair market value, not a bargain price.

Lease Term as a Percentage of Economic Life
The four-year lease is 80% of the five-year economic life, causing lease to be a capital lease.

Present Value of Lease Payments
$$PV = 10,522.85 \ (\text{PVIFA}_{.08,4})$$
$$= 10,522.85 \ (3.3121)$$
$$= 34,852.73$$

$$PV/MV = 34,852.73/40,000$$
$$= 0.8713$$

---

the lessee prior to lease expiration, the lease must necessarily be accounted for as a capital lease. In this case, such a transfer does not occur. Ownership of the truck will not change during the term of the lease.

The second test is whether or not there is a bargain purchase price involved at the expiration of the lease. In this case, the residual value of $7,000 is the best estimate of the fair market value at the end of the four-year period. Since this is the best estimate of fair market value, it does not constitute a bargain purchase option and the lease, at least according to this criteria, will not need to be recorded as a capital lease.

The third test involves the economic life of the asset. In this case we have an asset with a five-year economic life. The lease term is four years, that is, 80% of the economic life. This is greater than the 75% maximum outlined in SFAS No. 13. Thus, this lease must be accounted for as a capital lease, i.e., capitalized on the books of the lessee.

The third test automatically causes the lease to be capitalized. However, the fourth test also comes very close to qualifying the lease as a capital lease. There are four payments of $10,522.85, each payable at the end of the following four years. The present value of these payments at an 8% rate is $34,852.73 (using the PVIFA for 8% and four payments). This represents slightly over 87% of the value of the asset. The asset does not qualify under the fourth test, but the 87% result is quite close to the 90% cut-off and essentially confirms the appropriate treatment for this lease arrangement.

Since the lease is a capital lease, the accounting treatment is that the present value of the lease payments will become an asset on the books of the lessee and the present value of the lease payments (the identical amount) will be recorded as a liability. The two entries essentially offset each other having no net impact on the firm's capital, but simply increasing both the assets and the liabilities by the same amount.

FIGURE 6.5

Delivery Truck: Debt Amortization Schedule

Time	Interest[1]	Principal Reduction[2]	Unpaid Balance[3]
0	–	–	34,852.73
1	2,788.22	7,734.63	27,118.10
2	2,169.45	8,353.40	18,764.70
3	1,501.18	9,021.67	9,743.03
4	779.44	9,743.03[4]	0
	7,238.29	34,852.73	

[1] Represents 8% of previous unpaid balance.
[2] Represents payment of $10,522.85 minus applicable interest.
[3] Previous unpaid balance minus applicable principal reduction.
[4] The amount of the payment would suggest a principal reduction of $9,743.41. Difference is attributable to rounding.

Accounting Entries Each Year

Year		DR	CR
1	Interest expense	2,788.22	
	Capitalized lease liability	7,734.63	
	Cash		10,522.85
2	Interest expense	2,169.45	
	Capitalized lease liability	8,353.40	
	Cash		10,522.85
3	Interest expense	1,501.18	
	Capitalized lease liability	9,021.67	
	Cash		10,522.85
4	Interest expense	779.44	
	Capitalized lease liability	9,743.03	
	Cash		10,522.47

The Lease Liability and Its Amortization

The liability that appears on the books of the lessee will be amortized in the same way as any other long-term debt that appears on the balance sheet. The debt will be amortized at the 8% noted in Figure 6.3. The amortization schedule appears in Figure 6.5. In the amortization process, each of the equal payments is divided into two components – interest and principal reduction. Interest is computed on the unpaid balance prior to each payment.

For example, the unpaid balance for the delivery truck from time zero to time 1 is the full present value of all future lease payments, $34,852.73 (derived in Figure 6.4). At the rate of 8%, the interest on this amount for year 1 is $2,788.22 ($34,852.73 × 0.08). Since the total payment is $10,522.85, the amount by which the principal is reduced is $7,734.63 ($10,522.85 – $2,788.22). Thus, immediately after the first payment, the unpaid balance of the capitalized debt on the books of the lessee is $27,118.10 ($34,852.73 – $7,734.63). This remains the unpaid balance until the second payment is made.

The amount of interest in the second payment is 8% of the unpaid balance as of time 1 – $2,169.45 ($27,118.10 × 0.08). This is again subtracted from the annual installment of $10,522.85 to arrive at a principal reduction of $8,353.40 ($10,522.85 – $2,169.45). After the second payment, the unpaid balance is $18,764.70 ($27,118.10 – $8,353.40). This process continues until the balance is completely amortized. Notice that the total principal reduction column in Figure 6.5 equals the original amount of the liability and that the total interest in this case is $7,238.29.

Figure 6.5 also shows the exact accounting entries that should be made each year in order to record interest expense and the reduction in lease liability. Notice that each payment level is the same except for the fourth payment which is slightly smaller because of rounding differences in the amortization schedule.

FIGURE 6.6

Delivery Truck: Lease Amortization Schedule

Time	Amortization Expense	Unamortized Balance
0	–	34,852.73
1	8,713.18	26,139.55
2	8,713.18	17,426.37
3	8,713.18	8,713.19
4	8,713.19	0

Accounting Entries Each Year

	DR	CR
Amortization expense	8,713.18	
Capitalized lease asset		8,713.18

The Lease Asset and Its Amortization

The capitalized lease asset is also reduced each year. However, this amortization is typically done on a straight-line basis. The leased asset is amortized as a purchased asset would be depreciated. In this case, the asset of $34,852.73 is amortized on a straight-line basis at the rate of $8,713.18 per year.

The above sections describe the treatment of capital leases for accounting purposes. However, the method of accounting for a capital lease does not, in any way, affect the actual economic value of the lease.

THE ECONOMIC ANALYSIS OF A FINANCIAL LEASE

Whether or not the lease of an asset must be capitalized according to SFAS No. 13, the analysis of a proposed financial lease must be based on relevant cash flows. Note that all long-term, fixed-term leases of capital equipment may be considered financial leases. Capital leases are a subset of financial leases that meet the specific criteria outlined above. Other financial leases – that do not meet the capital lease criteria – may be structured to transfer certain benefits to lessee, such as depreciation of the asset. In either the capital lease case or the more generalized financial lease case, cash flow impact must be isolated:

- If the financial lease is to be capitalized, recording amortization expense is not associated with any cash outflow.

- If the financial lease is capitalized, there is no differential impact on cash flow from separating the payments into interest and principal reduction. Each payment reduces cash for the amount of the payment whether it is recorded as lease payment expense, or some combination of interest and principal reduction.

- If the financial lease is not capitalized, there may be an impact on tax liability that will impact cash flow. If taxing authorities consider the lease to be a form of financing to purchase an asset, only the interest portion of the lease payment – not the entire lease payment – will be tax-deductible. Since part of the payment (principal reduction) is not tax deductible, taxes will increase. Such an interpretation will have cash flow implications.

- If the financial lease is not capitalized, but is deemed a means of debt financing by taxing authorities, the lessee will be permitted to record depreciation expense associated with the leased asset. The tax-sheltering effect of depreciation expense – which is associated with no actual cash outflow – will at least partially offset the loss of deductibility of part of the lease payment.

FIGURE 6.7

Analysis of Financial Leases

- Cost of asset

- After-tax lease payments

- Forgone depreciation tax shield

- After-tax cost of debt as discount rate

- Net present value of lease

The Framework

Consider Figure 6.7, which assumes full tax-deductibility of lease payments and no depreciation expense associated with the leased asset. The important elements are outlined in evaluating an *outright purchase* versus a *financial lease*. The financial lease excludes cash flows normally associated with the asset in the traditional capital budgeting context, such as cost and depreciation tax shield. Instead, the analysis is focused on the cash flow differential between the decision to purchase a capital asset and the decision to lease the asset.

In this sense, the *cost of the asset* is a normal cash outflow that is no longer necessary if the asset is leased. This means that the acquisition cost of the asset will appear in the analysis at time zero as a positive cash flow – a forgone cash outflow.

The *lease payments* that are required under the agreement will be recorded as a negative cash flow. Assuming that these lease payments are fully tax-deductible, that is, the tax deductibility has not been lost because of certain characteristics of the lease contract, the after-tax lease payments will be reflected as negative cash flows in the time periods that are appropriate in the analysis.

If the asset is not purchased, but is instead leased, the lessee will lose the right to depreciate the asset. This means that it is necessary to record in the analysis the *forgone depreciation tax shield* when the asset is leased rather than purchased.

The net cash flows that are associated with the analysis must be discounted at an *after-tax cost of debt*, instead of the weighted average cost of capital. This is the appropriate rate to use because the financial lease is a form of debt. In addition, because each of the cash flows is analyzed on an after-tax basis, the cost of debt must also be stated on an after-tax basis.

The *net present value of the lease* is the present value of all future cash flows net of the initial cash flow at the time of lease initiation. If the net present value of the lease is positive, the lease option is superior to the purchase option. On the other hand, if the net present value of the lease is negative, the purchase option is superior.

Purchase Decision – Example

Figure 6.8 gives the details of a lease analysis example that will lead to selection of the purchase alternative. In this case, the equipment in question is a new computer system with an estimated life of four years, which is also the term of the lease. The annual lease payment that is required is

FIGURE 6.8	
Financial Leases: Computer Equipment	
Cost of new computer equipment ($)	100,000
Estimated economic life (years)	4
Term of lease (years)	4
Annual lease payment ($)	24,000
Cost of debt (%)	8
Number of lease payments	5
Tax rate (%)	34
NPV of new computer ($)[1]	11,600

[1] Includes the present value of the depreciation tax shield assuming straight-line depreciation (no salvage value) over four years.

$24,000. The lessee cost of borrowing in this case is the (pre-tax) interest rate of 8%. Under the terms of this lease, an initial payment of $24,000 is required at the time that the computer system is installed. For each of the four years that follow, another lease payment of $24,000 must be made.

When the computer equipment is analyzed under the assumption of equipment purchase, the project has a net present value of $11,600. Thus, the computer system itself is an acceptable project because its net present value is positive. The question is whether it is better to lease the equipment or to purchase it.

FIGURE 6.9

Computer Equipment: Net Present Value of Lease

	0	1	2	3	4
Cost	100,000				
After-tax lease payments[1]	(15,840)	(15,840)	(15,840)	(15,840)	(15,840)
Forgone depreciation tax shield[2]		(8,500)	(8,500)	(8,500)	(8,500)
	84,160	(24,340)	(24,340)	(24,430)	(24,340)

$$NPV = -24,340 \ (PVIFA_{0.0528,4}) + 84,160$$
$$= -24,340 \ (3.230) + 84,160$$
$$= -85,750 + 84,160$$
$$= -1,590$$

[1] $24,000 \ (1 - 0.34) = 15,840$

[2] $\left(\dfrac{100,000}{4} \right) (0.34) = 8,500$

The specific cash flows that are relevant for this lease analysis are shown in Figure 6.9. The first component is the cost of the system. This is a cost that will not be incurred if the equipment is leased and is shown as a positive $100,000 at the time of acquisition.

The second relevant cash flow is the after-tax lease payments. Assuming that 100% of the lease payments will be tax-deductible and that the appropriate tax rate is 34%, the after-tax lease payment is $15,840 ($15,840 × [1 − 0.34]). According to the terms of the lease, a payment must be made at the time that the equipment is placed into service and at the end of each of the four years.

The net present value of the equipment included a depreciation tax shield. It was assumed that the equipment would be depreciated using a straight-line method over four years. If the equipment is leased, the tax benefits of this depreciation will be lost. The annual amount of depreciation on this $100,000 investment over a four-year period is $25,000. Under the purchase alternative, this amount of income is shielded from taxation, creating a depreciation tax shield equal to the amount of the depreciation multiplied by the tax rate. In this case, the amount of the depreciation tax shield is $8,500. (See Chapter 4 for discussion of the calculation of the depreciation tax shield.) Since this tax shield will be forgone under the lease alternative, this amount is reflected as a negative amount in Figure 6.9.

When the present value of the future negative cash flows is combined with the net positive cash flow realized at the time of acquisition, the net present value of the lease is a −$1,590. In other words, this lease should not be accepted. The computer equipment should be purchased because the project is viable. But the terms of the lease are not favorable.

Adjusted Net Present Value – Purchase Decision

The concept of *adjusted net present value* includes both the net present value of the project and the net present value of the lease. Figure 6.10

FIGURE 6.10

Adjusted Net Present Value: Computer Equipment

ANPV = NPV of project + NPV of lease
= 11,600 − 1,590
= 10,010

---

illustrates this idea. The net present value of the computer system is $11,600 but the net present value of the lease is –$1,590, thus the leased asset has an adjusted net present value of $10,010.

Since the adjusted net present value ($10,010) is less than the net present value under the purchase option ($11,600), shareholder wealth is maximized by purchasing the system.

Lease Decision – Example

The example above can be modified slightly to illustrate the opposite case, that is, the case in which the lease has a positive net present but the

---

FIGURE 6.11

Net Present Value of Lease

	0	1	2	3	4
Cost	100,000				
After-tax lease payments[1]		(15,840)	(15,840)	(15,840)	(15,840)
Forgone depreciation tax shield[2]		(8,500)	(8,500)	(8,500)	(8,500)
	84,160	(24,340)	(24,340)	(24,340)	(8,500)

$$NPV = -24,340 \ (PVIFA_{0.528,3}) - 8,500 \ (PVIF_{0.0528,4}) + 84,160$$
$$= -24,340 \ (2.7090) - 8,500 \ (0.8140) + 84,160$$
$$= -65,937 - 6,919 + 84,160$$
$$= 11,304$$

[1] $24,000 \ (1 - 0.34) = 15,840$

[2] $\left(\dfrac{100,000}{4}\right)(0.34) = 8,500$

Note: This analysis is based on the information in Figure 6.8, with the exception that only four lease payments are required and the NPV of the new computer is –$2,500.

---

project does not. Figure 6.11 contains the same information that is contained in Figure 6.8, with two exceptions.

- There are four (not five) lease payments. The payment at the end of year 4 is no longer necessary.
- The net present value of the new computer is –$2,500. That is, the project is not viable under the purchase alternative.

All cash flows in Figure 6.11 are equivalent to those in Figure 6.9 with the exception of the number of after-tax cash flows that are attributable to lease payments. Because there is no lease payment at the end of year 4, the net cash flow for year 4 is –$8,500 (the forgone depreciation tax shield). The absence of a lease payment in year 4 causes the net present value of the lease to be positive, in this case, $11,304.

Adjusted Net Present Value – Lease Decision

Leasing is a better option than purchasing in this case. If the net present value of the project had been positive, the lease would have added to the overall positive net present value of the project. However, in this case, the net present value of the project is –$2,500. While the net present value of the project assuming purchase is negative, the net present value of the lease is positive. The adjusted net present value of the project is also positive. This means that the project will have a positive net present value of $8,804 *if, and only if, the equipment is leased.*

This is a case in which the form of financing has an important role to play in the decision with respect to project adoption.

FIGURE 6.12

Adjusted Net Present Value: Computer Equipment

$$ANPV = NPV \text{ of project} + NPV \text{ of lease}$$
$$= -2,500 + 11,304$$
$$= \underline{8,804}$$

Note: This analysis is based on the information in Figure 6.8, with the exception that only four lease payments are required and the NPV of the new computer is –$2,500.

SUMMARY

Lease financing is an important consideration when making a capital budgeting decision. Generally, a project should be analyzed without regard to financing. However, tax advantages of leasing or more favorable lease terms can sometimes cause a project to be more acceptable if the equipment is leased.

A capital lease is one that must be handled in a specific way, that is, it must be capitalized and appear on the balance sheet of the lessee. Both the asset and the liability that are recorded are amortized over the term of the lease. A lease must be accounted for as a capital lease if it meets at least one of the four tests set out in FASB No. 13, *Accounting for Leases*. These four tests involve:

- transfer of ownership
- a bargain purchase price
- length of the lease term
- present value of lease payments.

Financial leases are those that substitute as a form of long-term financing (with some also being classified as capital leases). The appropriate steps in analyzing a financial lease are first to analyze the project assuming that it will be purchased in the year of acquisition. All the customary rules of capital budgeting apply in computing the project's net present value. After the customary analysis, the lease itself should be considered. The net present value of the lease will depend on:

- cost of the asset
- after-tax lease payments
- forgone depreciation tax shield
- any other cash flows that are relevant to the lease only.

In some cases, a financial lease will not be acceptable because its net present value is negative. That is, it will be more advantageous to purchase the asset rather than to lease it. In other cases, a lease will actually add to the value of the project because the financing terms are favorable enough to offset a negative net present value under the purchase assumption. Of course, if both net present value of the project under the assumption of asset purchase and net present value under the assumption of asset lease are positive, the project should be accepted and the lease terms pursued.

6

THE TIME VALUE OF MONEY

INTRODUCTION

The cash flows that are used to determine value in a capital budgeting context are evaluated over long periods of time. This process necessitates consideration of the time value of money. This appendix outlines the concepts and illustrates the application of the time value of money.

INDIVIDUAL CASH FLOWS

The concept of the time value of money can be capsulized in one statement:

A dollar received today is worth more than a dollar received one year from today.

Expanding this logic, a given cash flow can be valued at any point in time. From a conceptual standpoint, the passage of time may be depicted by a *time line*. A time line begins with the current period – the current point in time – and identifies other points in time that are exactly one, two, three, four, or more years in the future. Each point on the time line indicates a specific moment. The space between these points indicates the passage of time.

Future Value

Figure A.1 illustrates both the time line and a specific cash flow. In this example, $100 is valued as of today, that is, time zero. A question that would correspond with this time line is, "If you deposited $100 in an account that paid 8% and then left the account untouched for five years, to what amount would the balance have grown at the end of five years?"

The answer is actually a series of steps. The first step is to determine the value of the deposit at the end of one year. The reason for this first step is that 8% is an annual interest rate, thus it is necessary to determine the balance in the account at the end of the first year. This is equivalent to asking

---

FIGURE A.1

The Future Value of a Single Amount

0	1	2	3	4	5
					$*$
100.00					?

$$FV_1 = 100.00\ (1.08) = 108.00$$
$$FV_2 = 108.00\ (1.08) = 116.64$$
$$FV_3 = 116.64\ (1.08) = 125.97$$
$$FV_4 = 125.97\ (1.08) = 136.05$$
$$FV_5 = 136.05\ (1.08) = 146.93$$

or

$$FV_5 = 100.00\ (1.08)^5 = 146.93$$

Future Value Interest Factor:
$$FVIF_{k,n} = (1 + k)^n$$
$$FVIF_{0.08,5} = (1.08)^5 = 1.469328$$

Future Value of a Single Amount:
$$FV_n = PV\ (1 + k)^n$$
$$= PV\ (FVIF_{k,n})$$

the question "What is the future value of $100 placed in an 8% account for one year?" The answer is $108 as shown in Figure A.1. That is, FV_1, the future value of $100 at the end of period 1, equals PV, present value of $100, multiplied by (1.08).

This process is repeated in year 2. The value at the end of year 2, that is, FV_2, equals $116.64. This is, of course, $108 multiplied by (1.08). This process continues for the next three years so that the future value at the end of period 5, that is, FV_5, is $146.93.

In other words, the future value at year 5, FV_5, equals $100 multiplied by $(1.08)^5$. The $100 original principal or PV is multiplied by the quantity (1.08) a total of five times. This relationship is standardized in the sense that the amount of interest and principle $(1 + k)$ has been identified as a specific multiplicative factor called *future value interest factor*, abbreviated as $FVIF_{k,n}$. The future value interest factor is identified as $(1 + k)^n$. As also indicated in Figure A.1, the future value interest factor for the combination of 8% and five years is $(1.08)^5$, or 1.469328.

When time value of money principles are generalized, the future value of a single amount can be specified by a relationship shown in Figure A.1. The future value of a single amount at any point on the time line may be found by multiplying the present value by the relevant FVIF. This relationship will always hold true and can be used in any case. The FVIF is a function of two variables – the rate of interest for the year and the number of years that are involved.

The valuation formula for the future value of a single amount is:

$$FV_n = PV(1 + k)^n = PV(FVIF_{k,n}) \tag{1}$$

Present Value

The example in the above section answers the question of how much an amount will grow to after five years if placed on deposit at a rate of 8%. It is also possible to use time value of money concepts to determine the amount one would be willing to pay today for a future payment, as shown in Figure A.2.

Assume now that the question is "How much would you be willing to pay today in exchange for the right to receive a cash flow of $200 at the end of five years if you required 8% on your investment?" This question is equivalent to "What is the present value of $200 at 8% for five years?" This situation still involves a single amount and the basic equation for the future value of a single amount. The difference is that the future value is known and the present value is not. As above, the rate of interest and the number of years are given. In this case, the present value equals the future value multiplied by the inverse of $(1 + k)^5$. Substituting $200 for the future value, 8% for k, and 5 for n, the present value is $136.12. In other words, an individual whose required rate of return is 8% would pay $136.12 in exchange for the right to receive $200 at the end of year 5.

FIGURE A.2

Present Value of a Single Amount

0	1	2	3	4	5
*					
?					200

$$FV_s = PV (1 + k)^5$$

$$PV (1 + k)^5 = FV_s$$

$$PV = FV_s \left(\frac{1}{(1 + k)^5} \right)$$

Substituting,

$$PV = 200 \left(\frac{1}{(1.08)^5} \right)$$

$$= 136.12$$

Present Value Interest Factor:

$$PVIF_{n,k} = \left(\frac{1}{(1 + k)^n} \right)$$

Present Value of a Single Amount:

$$PV = FV_n \left(\frac{1}{(1 + k)^n} \right)$$

$$= FV_n (PVIF_{k,n})$$

$$FV_n = PV(1 + k)^n = PV(FVIF_{k,n})$$

As was true with the future value problem, a standardized factor can be derived to determine the present value. This factor is called the *present value interest factor*. It is calculated as the *inverse of $(1 + k)^5$*. In this case, the PVIF is 0.680583.

In general, the future value equation is used to solve for the present value. Solving for present value means isolating present value on one side of the equal sign and placing all other terms on the other side of the equal sign.

The valuation formula for the present value of a single amount is:

$$PV = FV_n \left(\frac{1}{(1 + k)^n} \right) = FV_n (PVIF_{k,n}) \tag{2}$$

Implied Rate of Return

Up to this point, the formula in Figure A.1 has been used to find the future value and the present value of a single amount. It is also possible to use the

---

FIGURE A.3

Implied Rate of Return

0	1	2	3	4	5
*					
(400)					674.02

$$FV_s = PV (1 + k)^5$$
$$PV (1 + k)^5 = FV_s$$
$$(1 + k)^5 = (FV_s/PV)$$

Taking the fifth root of both sides,
$$(1 + k) = (FV_s/PV)^{1/5}$$
$$k = (FV_s/PV)^{1/5} - 1$$

Substituting,
$$k = (674.02/400)^{1/5} - 1$$
$$= (1.68505)^{1/5} - 1$$
$$= 0.10999$$
$$= 0.11$$

Implied Rate of Return:
$$FV_n = PV(1 + k)^n$$
$$k = (FV_n/PV)^{1/n} - 1$$

---

same formula and solve for *k*. The relevant question in this case is "What rate of return does an investor receive if the investor pays a specified price today in exchange for a promised payoff in the future?" Figure A.3 presents an example. The question that can be associated with this time line is "If an investor paid $400 for the right to receive $674.02 in five years, what rate of return would that investor expect on average each year?" The answer is the rate implied by the single-amount formula, with PV = $400, FV_s = $674.02, and *n* = 5.

Dividing both sides of the single-amount equation by PV, leaves $(1 + k)^5$. To solve for *k*, it is necessary to take the fifth root of both sides of the equation. In this way, the quantity $(1 + k)$ is isolated on the left-hand side of the equation.[1] When 1 is subtracted from both sides, the result is that the *implied rate of return*, or *k*, is $(FV_s/PV)^{1/5} - 1$. Substituting the values that are relevant here and solving for *k*, the implied rate of return is 11%. When this relationship is generalized, it is clear that the implied rate of return is a function of the future value, the present value, and the number of periods that elapses between them.

The formula for implied rate of return in the case of a single amount is:

$$k = \left(\frac{FV_n}{PV}\right)^{\frac{1}{n}} - 1 \qquad (3)$$

Notice that one equation has been used to satisfy three requirements. All of the problems have been solved using the formula for the future value of a single amount, varying only the unknown. In Figure A.1, the unknown was future value, in Figure A.2 it is present value, and in Figure A.3, it is implied rate of return.

---

[1] Whenever a quantity that already has been raised to a power (other than 1) is raised to another power, the powers or exponents are multiplied in order to arrive at the value of the quantity. In this case, raising both sides of the equation to the 1/5 power, or taking the fifth root, results in the left-hand side being raised to the power of 1.

Implied Rate of Return versus Required Rate of Return

In the examples above, two concepts of rate of return were employed. The first was a required rate of return, when k was specified as 8% in Figures A.1 and A.2. In both cases, 8% was given. The rate was a function of some external decision with respect to the appropriate rate of return. On the other hand, k was the unknown in Figure A.3. The differentiation is between *required rate of return* and *expected rate of return*.

Looking at it another way, Figure A.2 is an exercise that answers the question "What is the present value of a single amount?" This question can be restated as "What is the maximum that an investor should be willing to pay today in order to receive $200 at the end of five years *if 8% was the investor's minimum required rate of return*?" In both Figures A.1 and A.2, the external decision making with respect to the rate of return was completed beforehand. In an actual case, the rate of return is an extremely important factor that must be determined by the decision maker on the basis of the current interest rate environment and the risk involved in the project.

The first two cases are contrasted with the third case in which the rate of return is the unknown. In Figure A.3, the question is "What rate of return would an investor earn on average each year if the investor paid $400 today with the promise of receiving $674.02 in five years?" This rate of return is derived from given cash flows. It is not necessary to determine the risk of the project. In fact, the risk of the project is irrelevant to the calculation. This rate of return is a mathematical result – simply the rate that will cause the present value of $674.02 to equal $400 or the expected return.

> *The required rate of return must be based on some objective criterion and the expected rate of return will always be a function of the cash flows that are given.*

Point of Valuation

Implicit in the discussions thus far has been the concept of *point of valuation*. As noted above, the time line identifies points in time that occur 1, 2, 3, 4, or 5 years after today – time zero. Recall also that any cash flow may be valued anywhere along the time line. In the cases that we have used up to this point, the cash flow occurred either at time zero (future value calculation), time 5 (present value calculation), or both (implied rate of return).

Referring to Figure A.1, recall that the cash flow itself occurred at time zero but the question was "What is the value of that cash flow at time 5?" In this case, the point of valuation, or the point on the time at which the $100 was to be valued, was year 5.

Looking again at Figure A.2, the cash flow of $200 occurred at time 5. The question was "How much would an investor be willing to pay today, time zero?" In this example, time zero was a point valuation.

The point of valuation for a single amount is the point on the time line at which a cash flow is valued.

The interpretation of *n* in this exercise is the number of periods between the cash flow and the point of valuation. This point of valuation may occur anywhere along the time line.

INTRA-YEAR COMPOUNDING

Up to this point, all compounding has been on an annual basis, that is, interest has been computed only one time per year. *Intra-year compounding* involves compounding more than one time during the year. Figure A.4 is essentially the same case as in Figure A.1, with one exception – instead of 8% being paid each year, 4% is paid each six-month period.

FIGURE A.4

Intra-year Compounding: Future Value – Semi-annual Case

0	1	2	3	4	5
					*
100					?

$$FV_{0.5} = 100.00\,(1.04) = 104.00$$
$$FV_{1} = 104.00\,(1.04) = 108.16$$
$$FV_{1.5} = 108.16\,(1.04) = 112.49$$
$$FV_{2} = 112.49\,(1.04) = 116.99$$
$$FV_{2.5} = 116.99\,(1.04) = 121.67$$
$$FV_{3} = 121.67\,(1.04) = 126.54$$
$$FV_{3.5} = 126.54\,(1.04) = 131.60$$
$$FV_{4} = 131.60\,(1.04) = 136.86$$
$$FV_{4.5} = 136.86\,(1.04) = 142.33$$
$$FV_{5} = 142.33\,(1.04) = 148.02$$

As shown in Figure A.4, at the end of the first six months, the balance will have grown to $104. By the end of year 1, the balance is not $108 as in Figure A.1, but is instead $108.16. Each successive six-month period results in the compounding, or growth, of the balance at the rate of 4%. At the end of five years – again, the point of valuation is year 5 – the value of the account is $148.02.

Recall that with annual compounding (Figure A.1) over an equivalent five-year period at 8%, $100 grew to $146.93. The difference between these two amounts ($1.09) is interest on interest. Effectively, interest is earned earlier, is added to the balance, and begins earning interest sooner. It should be noted that interest on interest is also earned in the annual case, but that in the intra-year compounding case, the interest on interest accrues faster.

There are three new concepts that are applied when intra-year compounding is introduced.

- The *number of times per year interest is paid or compounded* is denoted by *m*. In the case of semiannual compounding, or compounding twice a year, the value of *m* is 2.

- The *rate of return per period* is also relevant. In the previous examples (Figures A.1–3), the rate of return was stated as an annual rate. While rates are always quoted on an annual basis even in an intra-year compounding case, the rate must be adjusted to the rate per period for the purposes of time value of money concepts. This adjustment is made by dividing *k* by *m* to arrive at the rate per period.

- The *number of periods* must be substituted for the number of years. For the previous example, the number of periods equaled the number of years. When intra-year compounding is used, this is not the case. The number of periods will be the number of years multiplied by the number of periods per year.

Figure A.5 shows the impact of intra-year compounding using the present value of $100 and an annual rate of 8% over a five-year period. The first two entries, annual and semiannual, were computed above and are presented for comparative purposes.

Essentially, when annual compounding applies and the rate of interest is 8% annually over five years, the future value interest factor is 1.469328 or $(1.08)^5$. In the case of semiannual compounding, the factor is adjusted so that 4% is the rate per period and the number of periods is 10, that is, the factor is computed as $(1.04)^{10}$. The result is that $100 grows to $148.02 rather than $146.93. When compounding frequency increases to four times per year – that is, quarterly – the rate of return per period decreases to 2% but the number of periods increases to 20. The result is that the future value is $148.59. On a monthly basis, the rate of return decreases to 0.6667% per period and the number of periods increases to 60. The future value then is $148.99. When the compounding frequency is daily, there are 365 compounding periods per year. Over a five-year period, this results in 1,825 periods but the rate per period is substantially smaller at 0.0219% per period. Accordingly, the future value increases to $149.13.

FIGURE A.5

Intra-year Compounding – Varying Intervals

Given: PV   =   100.00

           annual rate   =   0.08

           number of years   =   5

Compounding Frequency	m	$FVIF_{k,n}$	FV_5
Annual	1	$(1.08)^5 = 1.469328$	146.93
Semiannual	2	$(1.04)^{10} = 1.480244$	148.02
Quarterly	4	$(1.02)^{20} = 1.485947$	148.59
Monthly	12	$(1.006667)^{60} = 1.489875$	148.99
Daily	365	$(1.000219)^{1825} = 1.491275$	149.13

m =   number of times per year interest is compounded or paid

k =   annual rate/m

    =   rate per period

n =   (m)(number of years)

    =   number of periods

When computing future value, intra-year compounding causes the results to increase as the number of periods per year increases. Conversely, the more frequent the intra-year compounding, the smaller will be the results of present value calculations.

CONTINUOUS COMPOUNDING

The intra-year compounding that was discussed in the previous section, regardless of the frequency, is still considered *discreet compounding*. Discreet compounding means that the periods of time are measured with a beginning and ending point in time, even if the beginning and ending points are extremely close together.

On the other hand, when it is not possible to differentiate the beginning and ending of a compounding period, the method of compounding is said to be *continuous*. With continuous compounding, the interval over which interest is compounded is infinitely small. This compounding method requires a different form of the valuation formula for a single amount.

$$FV_n = PV(e^{kt}) \tag{4}$$

FIGURE A.6

Continuous Compounding – Future Value

0	1	2	3	4	5
					*
100					?

$$FV_n \ = \ PV(e^{kt})$$

Substituting

$$FV_5 \ = \ 100\ (e^{(0.08)(5)})$$
$$= \ 100\ (e^{0.40})$$
$$= \ 100\ (1.491825)$$
$$= \ 149.18$$

Future Value

The formula and its application are illustrated in Figure A.6, using the example of a $100 deposit at 8% for five years. The question once again is "What is the future value of the $100 at 8%?" However, because it is impossible to identify specific periods and rate per period (because of the shortness of the compounding intervals), the future value must be respecified. The future value at period *n* equals the present value multiplied by e^{kt}, where *e* is the natural logarithm function with the value of 2.718281828, *k* is the appropriate annual rate, and *t* is the number of years that apply. In most cases, this function will be included on a financial or scientific calculator as the key e^x. It is not possible to perform this continuous compounding equation without either using a preprogrammed calculator key, e^x, or the base equivalent of 2.718281828.

Although the example in Figure A.6 may be done either way, the preprogrammed calculator approach is demonstrated. Substituting $100 for present value, 0.08 for *k*, and 5 for *t*, $100 \times e^{0.40} = 100$ times 1.491825. The result is that the future value at 5 is $149.18. This is the highest future value that can be obtained at 8% over five years. Notice that it is even greater than the daily compounding result by 5 cents. Thus, the range of values for the future value of $100 at 8% over five years is between $146.93–$149.18. This range directly relates to the frequency of compounding – from annual compounding to continuous compounding. All other compounding frequencies will yield results that fall within this range.

Present Value

Figure A.7 illustrates the use of continuous compounding to find present values. As was the case with the example in Figure A.2, the question is "What is the maximum that an investor would be willing to pay today in order to receive $200 in five years if the minimum required rate of return was 8%?" In this case, the question is qualified by stipulating continuous compounding. The future value formula using continuous compounding is used to solve for present value. That is, present value is isolated on the left-hand side of the equation while all other terms are isolated on the other side of the equation.

$$PV = FV_n \left(\frac{1}{e^{kt}} \right) \tag{5}$$

FIGURE A.7

Continuous Compounding – Present Value

0	1	2	3	4	5
*					
?					200

$$FV_n = PV(e^{kt})$$

$$PV\,(e^{kt}) = FV_n$$

$$PV = FV_n \left(\frac{1}{e^{kt}} \right)$$

Substituting,

$$PV = 200 \left(\frac{1}{e^{(0.08)(5)}} \right)$$

$$= 200 \left(\frac{1}{1.4918247} \right)$$

$$= 200\,(0.670320)$$

$$= 134.06$$

Substituting the specific values in this problem, present value equals $200 multiplied by 0.670320 or $134.06. Notice that the difference between the results of Figure A.7 to the results of Figure A.2 is $2.06 (136.12 – 134.06). When continuous compounding is applied, it is necessary to invest $2.06 less to obtain a $200 payoff in year 5 as compared to annual compounding.

Implied Rate of Return

Figure A.8 illustrates the application of the implied rate of return using continuous compounding. The example is parallel to that in Figure A.3, that is, a $400 payment in exchange for $674.02 to be received in five years. The equation is the same as that used in Figures A.6 and A.7, FV = PV(e^{kt}). The difference between this approach and that used in Figure A.3 is the way in which k is determined. The equation again must be solved

---

FIGURE A.8

Continuous Compounding – Implied Rate of Return

0	1	2	3	4	5
*					
(400)					674.02

$$FV_n = PV(e^{kt})$$
$$PV(e^{kt}) = FV_n$$
$$e^{kt} = FV_n/PV$$
$$k = \ln(FV_n/PV)/t$$

where $\ln(FV_n/PV) =$ natural log of FV_n/PV
$$= kt$$

Substituting,

$$e^{kt} = 674.02/400$$
$$= 1.685050$$

$$\ln(1.685050) = 0.521795$$
$$= k(5)$$
$$k = 0.521795/5$$
$$= 0.104359$$

---

so that k is isolated on one side of the equation while all other terms are isolated on the other side.

Now k is a part of the exponent of base e. It is necessary to find the natural log of FV_n/PV and then solve for k. It is necessary at this point to use a natural log key, often indicated as LN on financial calculators. Unlike the future value and present value cases, in which it is possible to arrive at the solution using the numerical value of e, it is not possible to identify the implied rate of return in any way other than using the natural log (LN) function of a calculator.

The process is to enter the ratio of future value to present value and activate the natural log key. When this is done the result is the specific exponent of e (kt) that will cause e^{kt} to equal the ratio of FV_n/PV. This exponent (the log of the ratio of future value to present value) then actually represents the product of the rate of return and the number of years. Notice in this case that the rate of return will be the annual rate and that t is the number of years. The concept of number of periods within a year has no meaning in continuous compounding because the intervals are infinitely small. Thus, all periods are stated in number of years and all rates are stated on an annual basis.

Substituting the values that apply in this example, we find that e^{kt} equals 1.685050. First entering this value and then finding its natural log results in a value of 0.521795. This number is interpreted as k multiplied by 5 (the number of years). In other words, it is 5 times the annual rate of return. Dividing this number by 5 yields the annual rate of 0.104359 or 10.44%.

Comparing this result to the result in Figure A.3 illustrates the impact of using continuous compounding or intra-year compounding versus annual compounding. In the case of continuous compounding, the expected annual rate of return is 10.44%. In the case of annual compounding the expected return is 11.00%. This is interpreted to mean that, on a continuous basis, the rate of return that is required to cause $400 to grow to $674.02 is lower than the rate of return that is necessary when that amount is compounded on an annual basis. This generally will be the case – a lower rate of return will achieve the same results when continuous compounding is used vis-à-vis annual compounding.

GENERAL CONCEPTS

The same logic extends generally to intra-year compounding, as well. Whenever intra-year compounding is used and the results compared with annual compounding, certain general results can be expected.

- When the future value is computed using intra-year or continuous compounding, the result will be greater than the future value found using annual compounding.

- When intra-year or continuous compounding is used to find the present value of a single amount, the present value will be lower or smaller than the result that will be obtained when annual compounding is used.

- In finding the expected rate of return when intra-year or continuous compounding is used, the rate will be lower than that obtained when the calculation assumes annual compounding.

In each case, a basic formula will apply. In the case of discreet compounding, that formula is the future value interest factor of a single amount. It is the formula that is contained in Figure A.1:

$$FV_n = PV(1 + k)^n$$

This formula can be manipulated or changed depending upon the variable that is unknown. It can be used to find future value, present value, or implied rate of return.

In the case of continuous compounding, the basic equation is contained in Figure A.6:

$$FV_n = PVe^{kt}$$

This equation can be used to find future value, present value, and implied or expected rate of return.

ANNUITIES

Up to this point, only single amounts have been valued at various points along the time line. Time value of money concepts may also be applied to multiple cash flows. Annuities, defined in Figure A.9, are an important subset of multiple cash flows. As long as cash flows meet these criteria, those cash flows constitute an annuity. This set of criteria stipulates that the cash flows must be equal in amount, with equal intervals between them, and that there must be a finite number of cash flows. When these conditions are met, there are certain concepts that make the process of finding the value of these multiple cash flows more efficient.

FIGURE A.9

Defining an Annuity

As long as the following conditions are met, a set of multiple cash flows constitutes an annuity:

- a series of cash flows
- cash flows of equal amount
- equal interval between cash flows
- a finite number of cash flows.

Future Value

Figure A.10 is an example of an annuity with five cash flows, each in the amount of $100. Because each cash flow is identical, the cash flows are identified as specific cash flows that apply to a specific year. For example, CF_1 is the cash flow in year 1. The first example of an annuity asks the question "What would be the balance in an account in which $100 is invested in each of the next five years, beginning one year from now, if the account earns 8%, compounded annually?" The point of valuation is assumed to be immediately after the last deposit is made. In essence, the

FIGURE A.10

Future Value of an Annuity

0	1	2	3	4	5
					*
	100	100	100	100	100
	CF_1	CF_2	CF_3	CF_4	CF_5
					?

$$
\begin{aligned}
FV &= CF_1(1.08)^4 + CF_2(1.08)^3 + CF_3(1.08)^2 + CF_4(1.08)^1 + CF_5(1.08)^0 \\
&= 100[(1.08)^4 + (1.08)^3 + (1.08)^2 + (1.08)^1 + (1.08)^0] \\
&= 100\ [1.360489 + 1.259712 + 1.1664 + 1.08 + 1] \\
&= 100\ [5.866601] \\
&= 586.66
\end{aligned}
$$

$$
\begin{aligned}
FV_n &= CF\left(\sum_{t=1}^{n} (1+k)^t\right) \\
&= CF(FVIFA_{k,n})
\end{aligned}
$$

$$\text{where} \quad FVIFA_{k,n} = [(1+k)^n - 1]/k$$

point of valuation can be assumed to coincide with the last cash flow but would include valuation of the fifth cash flow.

The value of the annuity is the sum of the values of the individual cash flows. Thus, the problem may be restated as one in which it is necessary to find the future value of each of the five individual payments. The future value of the first cash flow, CF_1, is determined by compounding this amount for four periods. Four periods is the appropriate number of periods for CF_1 because four years elapse between the point of valuation (year 5) and the cash flow (year 1). Likewise, the appropriate number of periods to compound CF_2 is 3 because three years elapse between the cash flow (year 2) and the point of valuation (year 5). Using the same logic, each successive cash flow is compounded for one less period.

When $100 is substituted for each of the cash flows, that constant value may be factored out of each term on the right-hand side of the equation. What remains within the brackets on the right-hand side of the equation is a series of terms, each equal to (1.08) raised to the appropriate power. Notice that the last factor is raised to the power of zero. This is because the cash flow is received and immediately valued. Since no time passes between the time of the cash flow and the time of valuation, there is no increase in the value of CF_5 and it is worth $100.

What is left in the bracket is the sum of individual future value interest factors (FVIFs), equal to 5.866601. Multiplying this factor by $100, the future value of this annuity is $586.66. The answer to the question shows that the five $100 cash flows will be worth more than $500 in principal because the first four cash flows compound and earn interest, although the last cash flow does not.

This example can be generalized into the future value of an annuity, where the future value is the cash flow multiplied by the sum of the relevant single amount factors. This sum of relevant single amount future value interest factors has also been standardized into a factor called the *future value interest factor of an annuity*, $FVIFA_{k,n}$. In addition, the sum of the single amount factors, or $FVIFA_{k,n,}$ converges to the closed-form equation in Figure A.10:

$$FVIFA_{k,n} = \left(\frac{(1 + k)^n - 1}{k} \right)$$

(6)

Present Value

The approach for finding the present value of the same annuity is illustrated in Figure A.11. In this case, the question might be "What is the maximum amount that an investor would be willing to pay today to receive five annual $100 payments, with the first occurring one year from today, if 8% is the investor's minimum required rate of return?" This requires finding the present value of each of the individual cash flows. In this case, CF_1 is discounted at 8% for one period because there is one period between the point of valuation (year 0) and the cash flow (year 1).

FIGURE A.11

Present Value of an Annuity

0	1	2	3	4	5
*					
	100	100	100	100	100
	CF_1	CF_2	CF_3	CF_4	CF_5
?					

$$PV = CF_1 \left(\frac{1}{1.08}\right) + CF_2 \left(\frac{1}{(1.08)^2}\right) + CF_3 \left(\frac{1}{(1.08)^3}\right) + CF_4 \left(\frac{1}{(1.08)^4}\right) + CF_5 \left(\frac{1}{(1.08)^5}\right)$$

$$= 100 \left[\frac{1}{(1.08)} + \frac{1}{(1.08)^2} + \frac{1}{(1.08)^3} + \frac{1}{(1.08)^4} + \frac{1}{(1.08)^5} \right]$$

$$= 100\ [0.925926 + 0.857339 + 0.793832 + 0.735030 + 0.670583]$$

$$= 100\ [3.99271]$$

$$= 399.27$$

$$PV = CF \left(\sum_{t=1}^{n} \frac{1}{(1 + k)^t} \right)$$

$$= CF\ (PVIFA_{k,n})$$

where $PVIFA_{k,n} = [1 - 1/(1 + k)^n]/k$

Cash flow is discounted for two years because there are two periods between the point of valuation (year 0) and the cash flow (year 2). Each successive cash flow is discounted for one more year.

As was true in the previous example, $100 is substituted and then factored out of each term on the right-hand side of the equation. This leaves within the brackets the individual single amount present value factors using 8% for years 1–5. The sum of these factors is 3.99271 and the value of the annuity is $399.27.

The generalized formula for the present value of an annuity is CF multiplied by the sum of the relevant PVIFs or CF multiplied by $PVIFA_{k,n}$. $PVIFA_{k,n}$ also converges to a closed form equation:

$$\text{PVIFA}_{k,n} = \left(\dfrac{1 - \dfrac{1}{(1+k)^n}}{k} \right) \tag{7}$$

INTERPRETING FACTORS

There are *implied points of valuation* built into the annuity factors, and into the financial functions of hand-held calculators and spreadsheet programs. The implied points of valuation must be understood in order to apply the factors correctly or to use the built-in functions properly.

> *In the case of the future value interest factor of an annuity, the factor yields a value for the annuity that is valid only for the point on the time line that coincides exactly with last cash flow.*

In other words, if year 5 had not been the point of valuation according to the stated problem, then it would not have been possible to sum the individual factors to arrive at the closed-form annuity factor that is defined in Figure A.10 and equation 6.

Likewise, in Figure A.11, if the point of valuation of the problem had not been year zero, that is, one year prior to CF_1, it would not have been possible to arrive at the exact annuity factor that corresponds with the closed-form factor in Figure A.11 and equation 7.

> *In the case of the present value interest factor of an annuity, the factor yields a value for the annuity that is valid only for the point on the time line that is one period before the first cash flow.*

$\text{FVIFA}_{k,n}$ assumes a point of valuation that corresponds with the last cash flow. $\text{PVIFA}_{k,n}$ assumes a point of valuation that is one period before the first cash flow.

The *number of periods* is different in analyzing annuity factors versus single amount factors. The interpretation of *n in a single amount factor*, as noted earlier, is the *number of periods that elapse between the cash flow and the point of valuation*. In the case of an annuity, this definition has little meaning because there is one implied point of valuation but multiple cash flows. The proper interpretation of *n for an annuity factor* is the *number of cash flows in the annuity*. This means that application of the annuity factor for a five-year annuity will yield the same value regardless of which five years are involved.

	FIGURE A.12	

Interpreting Factors

	Interpretation for	
Variable	**Single amount**	**Annuity**
n	Number of periods between POV and CF	Number of CFs
Implied POV	None	For FVIFA, coincides with last CF
		For PVIFA, one period before first CF

Notes:
CF means cash flow
POV means point of valuation

Figure A.12 summarizes the important concepts to remember when applying single amount and annuity factors. For a single amount factor, there is *no implied* point of valuation. There is only a point of valuation according to the specific scenario. For example, a cash flow of $100 may be valued *anywhere* along the time line. The determination of *n* will depend entirely on the specific situation.

On the other hand, in the case of annuities, there is an *implied* point of valuation for both future value and present value factors. For the future value interest factor of an annuity, the implied point of valuation coincides exactly with the last cash flow in the annuity. For the present value interest factor of an annuity, the point of valuation is one period before the first cash flow in the annuity. In the event that the actual point of valuation that is stipulated by the specific scenario does not match the implied point of valuation, certain adjustments must be made.

FIGURE A.13

Example for Interpreting Future Value Annuity Factors

0	1	2	3	4	5	6	7	8
								*
	100	100	100	100	100			
								?

$$FV_5 = 100[FVIFA_{0.08,5}]$$
$$= 100[(1.08)^5 - 1)/0.08]$$
$$= 100[5.866601]$$
$$= 586.66$$

$$FV_8 = FV_5[FVIFA_{0.08,3}]$$
$$= 586.66 [(1.08)^3]$$
$$= 586.66 [1.259712]$$
$$= 739.02$$

Figure A.13 is an example of the case in which the implied point of valuation for a factor differs from the point of valuation stipulated by a specific scenario. Once again, this is a five-year annuity of $100 that begins one year from today. However, in this case, the question is "How much is this annuity worth at the end of year 8?" A possible scenario associated with this time line might be a series of payments into an investment vehicle for retirement – through year 5 – but the inability to withdraw any of the funds without tax penalty until year 8.

It is still possible to use the future value interest factor of an annuity, but it is also necessary to adjust the FVIFA result. When FVIFA for a five-year annuity at 8% is multiplied by $100, the result is once again $586.66, a value that is a correct as of the end of year 5 (see also Figure A.10). But if the funds are not to be used until year 8, they will be allowed to continue to compound for the next three years. The question is not how much the annuity is worth at the end of year 5, but rather how much it will be worth at the end of year 8?

At the end of year 5, the annuity is equivalent to the single amount of $586.66. Multiplying this amount by the FVIF for 8% and 3 years, yields the final result of $739.02. Three years is used for the single amount factor FVIF because the annuity has been reduced to $586.66 as of year 5. Since the point of valuation according to the scenario is year 8, the difference of three years requires use of $n = 3$. An investor with a required return of 8% would be indifferent between:

- receiving the five-year annuity;
- receiving $586.66 at the end of year 5.

FIGURE A.14

Example for Interpreting Present Value Annuity Factors

0	1	2	3	4	5	6	7	8	9	10
		*								
						100	100	100	100	100
		?								

$$PV_5 = 100[PVIFA_{0.08,5}]$$
$$= 100[(1 - 1/(1.08)^5)/0.08]$$
$$= 100[3.99271]$$
$$= 399.27$$

$$PV_2 = 399.27\ [PVIF_{0.08,3}]$$
$$= 399.27\ [1/(1.08)^3]$$
$$= 399.27\ [0.793832]$$
$$= 316.95$$

Likewise, a present value annuity problem may require an adjustment that is related to the point of valuation. For example, Figure A.14 also shows a five-year, $100 annuity. However, in this case, the first cash flow in the annuity does not occur until year 6. In addition, the point of valuation that is of interest in the problem is year 2. One possible scenario that might correspond with this time line is an investment that will return five payments that begin six years from now but return nothing in the earlier years. Furthermore, the investment may not be available or ready for investment for two years. So the question is, "Given these future payments, what will they be worth two years from today?"

Applying the present value interest factor of an annuity to the $100 cash flows, that is, multiplying $100 by the PVIFA for the combination of 8% and five years, again produces the result of $399.27 (see also Figure A.11). Because of the rule with respect to implied point of valuation, this amount is the value of the annuity as of year 5 (one year before the first cash flow). Since the requirement is to determine the value as of year 2, this amount must be discounted for three years. The annuity effectively has been reduced to a single amount that is a valid estimate of value as of at year 5. At the same time, the problem at-hand requires valuation at year 2. Since there are three periods between the restated cash flow (year 5) and the point of valuation according to the scenario (year 2), n for the PVIF is 3.

These examples illustrate the use of both annuity and single amount factors as applicable. It should be remembered that the annuity factors have special interpretations of implied point of valuation and number of periods. With these stipulations in mind, the future value of an annuity may be expressed as:

$$FV = CF(FVIFA_{k,n}) \tag{8}$$

$$\text{where } FVIFA_{k,n} = \left(\frac{(1 + k)^n - 1}{k} \right)$$

The present value of an annuity can be expressed as:

$$PV = CF(PVIFA_{k,n}) \tag{9}$$

where $\text{PVIFA}_{k,n} = \left(\dfrac{1 - \dfrac{1}{(1 + k)^n}}{k} \right)$

FINANCIAL CALCULATORS

A number of hand-held calculators will perform the functions illustrated in this chapter for single amounts and annuities. In the case of a *single amount*, there are four variables that must be considered:

- number of periods
- interest rate
- present value
- future value.

Only one of these may be an unknown variable; three are entered into the calculator, the calculator is programmed to compute the fourth.

In the case of *annuities*, there are two possible combinations. In each case there are four variables. The first case is future value of an annuity and the variables are:

- interest rate
- number of periods
- payment
- future value.

The second case is present value of annuity and the variables are:

 second case is present value of annuity and the variables are:

- interest rate
- number of periods
- payment
- present value.

Again, no more than one of these may be left as an unknown.

FIGURE A.15

Financial Calculator Example – Future Value of an Annuity

0	1	2	3	4	5	6	7	8
								*
	100	100	100	100	100			
								?

Keystroke		Display
f		FIN [To clear previous entries]
100	PMT	100.000000
8	i	8.000000
5	n	5.000000
	FV	−586.660096
f	FIN	−586.660096 [To clear]
	PV	−586.660096
8	i	8.00000000
3	n	3.00000000
	FV	739.022763

Note: This example uses the Hewlett-Packard 12C. Other financial calculator applications will differ slightly depending on the model.

Figure A.15 illustrates the application of hand held calculator techniques for the problem previously illustrated in Figure A.13. It is a five-year, $100 annuity at 8% that is to be valued as of year 8. The first step is to clear all registers of a calculator. Then the payment, interest rate, and number of payments are entered as shown. Once these three variables have been input, the command for calculation of future value is registered by pressing the FV key. Notice that the display will show the future value of $586.66. This is equivalent to the application of the future value interest factor of an annuity formula, which is the formula that financial calculators use. Notice that there is no indication on the calculator's display that this is a value as of year 5. Nevertheless, it coincides exactly to the previous calculations of FV$_5$. It is necessary for the user to understand this implied point of valuation. This completes the first half of the problem.

The second half of the problem is to value the annuity as of year 8. The $586.66 amount now becomes the present value. But before the calculation can be performed, the registers must be cleared once again. This part of the operation involves a single amount ($586.66) and will not require the use of the payment key. Instead, the amount of $586.66 is input as present value. The interest rate and number of periods are input and the command for future value registered. As found earlier, the future value is $739.02.

FIGURE A.16

Financial Calculator Example – Present Value of an Annuity

0	1	2	3	4	5	6	7	8	9	10
		*								
						100	100	100	100	100
		?								

Keystroke		Display
f	FIN	[To clear previous entries]
100	PMT	100.000000
8	i	8.000000
5	n	5.000000
	PV	–399.271004
f	FIN	–399.271004 [To clear]
	FV	–399.271004
8	i	8.00000000
3	n	3.00000000
	PV	316.954196

Note: This example uses the Hewlett-Packard 12C. Other financial calculator applications will differ slightly depending on the model.

The present value of the five-year, $100 annuity that begins in year 6 but must be valued as of year 2 is shown in Figure A.16, corresponding to the earlier example in Figure A.14. Again, the financial registers must be cleared. Once that has been done, the interest, number of periods, and payment are input. The command is registered for the present value of the annuity. The result is $399.27 as was the case in Figure A.14. The annuity problem has now been reduced to a single amount problem, completing the first half of the problem.

The registers are cleared once again and the $399.27 is input as the future value. The interest rate of 8% and the number of periods (3) are input and the command for present value is registered. As was the case in the earlier calculation, the present value is $316.95.

Combinations of present value, future value, single amount, and annuities are easily accommodated on hand-held calculators with financial functions. However, the user must understand the nature of the calculations and the assumptions that have been built into the programming of such calculators.

It also should be noted that when future values are input either as single amounts or annuities, present values will be computed by financial calculators and associated with the opposite algebraic sign. Likewise, when present values are input, future values and annuities will be computed by the calculators and associated with the opposite algebraic sign. The reasoning for such programming is that it is illogical both to receive a future cash flow (i.e., realize a positive cash flow in the future), and to receive a positive cash flow at the present time. This would be equivalent to suggesting that one could receive a cash payment today and also receive cash payments in the future. Instead, one either makes a payment today and receives payment in the future or vice versa.

This logic also follows when using financial calculators to compute an expected rate of return. In this case, the present value, future value (or amount of each future payment), and number of periods are input and the command is registered to find the interest rate. If both the present value and the future value (or amount of each future payment) have the same sign, an error message will generally be received.

SUMMARY

The time value of money is an important element in the capital budgeting process. It begins with a basic understanding of the premise that dollars received today are more valuable than dollars received in the future. The concepts also encompass measurement of rates of return for stated cash flows and valuation of multiple cash flow streams. There are a number of preprogrammed, hand-held calculators. In any event, the proper application of these concepts requires a clear understanding of the timing of actual cash flows and points of valuation (both implied and stated). The process of capital budgeting hinges on the appropriate application of these concepts.

PRESENT VALUE AND FUTURE VALUE FACTORS

Future Value of $1

■

Future Value of an Annuity of $1

■

Present Value of $1

■

Present Value of an Annuity of $1

Future Value of $1

$$FVIF = (1 + k)^n$$

Periods	1%	2%	3%	4%	5%	6%	7%	8%	9%	10%
1	1.0100	1.0200	1.0300	1.0400	1.0500	1.0600	1.0700	1.0800	1.0900	1.1000
2	1.0201	1.0404	1.0609	1.0816	1.1025	1.1236	1.1449	1.1664	1.1881	1.2100
3	1.0303	1.0612	1.0927	1.1249	1.1576	1.1910	1.2250	1.2597	1.2950	1.3310
4	1.0406	1.0824	1.1255	1.1699	1.2155	1.2625	1.3108	1.3605	1.4116	1.4641
5	1.0510	1.1041	1.1593	1.2167	1.2763	1.3382	1.4026	1.4693	1.5386	1.6105
6	1.0615	1.1262	1.1941	1.2653	1.3401	1.4185	1.5007	1.5869	1.6771	1.7716
7	1.0721	1.1487	1.2299	1.3159	1.4071	1.5036	1.6058	1.7138	1.8280	1.9487
8	1.0829	1.1717	1.2668	1.3686	1.4775	1.5938	1.7182	1.8509	1.9926	2.1436
9	1.0937	1.1951	1.3048	1.4233	1.5513	1.6895	1.8385	1.9990	2.1719	2.3579
10	1.1046	1.2190	1.3439	1.4802	1.6289	1.7908	1.9672	2.1589	2.3674	2.5937
11	1.1157	1.2434	1.3842	1.5395	1.7103	1.8983	2.1049	2.3316	2.5804	2.8531
12	1.1268	1.2682	1.4258	1.6010	1.7959	2.0122	2.2522	2.5182	2.8127	3.1384
13	1.1381	1.2936	1.4685	1.6651	1.8856	2.1329	2.4098	2.7196	3.0658	3.4523
14	1.1495	1.3195	1.5126	1.7317	1.9799	2.2609	2.5785	2.9372	3.3417	3.7975
15	1.1610	1.3459	1.5580	1.8009	2.0789	2.3966	2.7590	3.1722	3.6425	4.1772
16	1.1726	1.3728	1.6047	1.8730	2.1829	2.5404	2.9522	3.4259	3.9703	4.5950
17	1.1843	1.4002	1.6528	1.9479	2.2920	2.6928	3.1588	3.7000	4.3276	5.0545
18	1.1961	1.4282	1.7024	2.0258	2.4066	2.8543	3.3799	3.9960	4.7171	5.5599
19	1.2081	1.4568	1.7535	2.1068	2.5270	3.0256	3.6165	4.3157	5.1417	6.1159
20	1.2202	1.4859	1.8061	2.1911	2.6533	3.2071	3.8697	4.6610	5.6044	6.7275
25	1.2824	1.6406	2.0938	2.6658	3.3864	4.2919	5.4274	6.8485	8.6231	10.8347
30	1.3478	1.8114	2.4273	3.2434	4.3219	5.7435	7.6123	10.0627	13.2677	17.4494
35	1.4166	1.9999	2.8139	3.9461	5.5160	7.6861	10.6766	14.7853	20.4140	28.1024
40	1.4889	2.2080	3.2620	4.8010	7.0400	10.2857	14.9745	21.7245	31.4094	45.2593
45	1.5648	2.4379	3.7816	5.8412	8.9850	13.7646	21.0025	31.9204	48.3273	72.8905
50	1.6446	2.6916	4.3839	7.1067	11.4674	18.4202	29.4570	46.9016	74.3575	117.3909

11%	12%	13%	14%	15%	16%	17%	18%	19%	20%	Periods
1.1100	1.1200	1.1300	1.1400	1.1500	1.1600	1.1700	1.1800	1.1900	1.2000	1
1.2321	1.2544	1.2769	1.2996	1.3225	1.3456	1.3689	1.3924	1.4161	1.4400	2
1.3676	1.4049	1.4429	1.4815	1.5209	1.5609	1.6016	1.6430	1.6852	1.7280	3
1.5181	1.5735	1.6305	1.6890	1.7490	1.8106	1.8739	1.9388	2.0053	2.0736	4
1.6851	1.7623	1.8424	1.9254	2.0114	2.1003	2.1924	2.2878	2.3864	2.4883	5
1.8704	1.9738	2.0820	2.1950	2.3131	2.4364	2.5652	2.6996	2.8398	2.9860	6
2.0762	2.2107	2.3526	2.5023	2.6600	2.8262	3.0012	3.1855	3.3793	3.5832	7
2.3045	2.4760	2.6584	2.8526	3.0590	3.2784	3.5115	3.7589	4.0214	4.2998	8
2.5580	2.7731	3.0040	3.2519	3.5179	3.8030	4.1084	4.4355	4.7854	5.1598	9
2.8394	3.1058	3.3946	3.7072	4.0456	4.4114	4.8068	5.2338	5.6947	6.1917	10
3.1518	3.4785	3.8359	4.2262	4.6524	5.1173	5.6240	6.1759	6.7767	7.4301	11
3.4985	3.8960	4.3345	4.8179	5.3503	5.9360	6.5801	7.2876	8.0642	8.9161	12
3.8833	4.3635	4.8980	5.4924	6.1528	6.8858	7.6987	8.5994	9.5964	10.6993	13
4.3104	4.8871	5.5348	6.2613	7.0757	7.9875	9.0075	10.1472	11.4198	12.8392	14
4.7846	5.4736	6.2543	7.1379	8.1371	9.2655	10.5387	11.9737	13.5895	15.4070	15
5.3109	6.1304	7.0673	8.1372	9.3576	10.7480	12.3303	14.1290	16.1715	18.4884	16
5.8951	6.8660	7.9861	9.2765	10.7613	12.4677	14.4265	16.6722	19.2441	22.1861	17
6.5436	7.6900	9.0243	10.5752	12.3755	14.4625	16.8790	19.6733	22.9005	26.6233	18
7.2633	8.6128	10.1974	12.0557	14.2318	16.7765	19.7484	23.2144	27.2516	31.9480	19
8.0623	9.6463	11.5231	13.7435	16.3665	19.4608	23.1056	27.3930	32.4294	38.3376	20
13.5855	17.0001	21.2305	26.4619	32.9190	40.8742	50.6578	62.6686	77.3881	95.3962	25
22.8923	29.9599	39.1159	50.9502	66.2118	85.8499	111.0647	143.3706	184.6753	237.3763	30
38.5749	52.7996	72.0685	98.1002	133.1755	180.3141	243.5035	327.9973	440.7006	590.6682	35
65.0009	93.0510	132.7816	188.8835	267.8635	378.7212	533.8687	750.3783	1.05e+03	1.47e+03	40
109.5302	163.9876	244.6414	363.6791	538.7693	795.4438	1.17e+03	1.72e+03	2.51e+03	3.66e+03	45
184.5648	289.0022	450.7359	700.2330	1.08e+03	1.67e+03	2.57e+03	3.93e+03	5.99e+03	9.10e+03	50

Future Value of an Annuity of $1

$$\text{FVIFA} = [(1 + k)^n - 1]/k$$

Periods	1%	2%	3%	4%	5%	6%	7%	8%	9%	10%
1	1.0000	1.0000	1.0000	1.0000	1.0000	1.0000	1.0000	1.0000	1.0000	1.0000
2	2.0100	2.0200	2.0300	2.0400	2.0500	2.0600	2.0700	2.0800	2.0900	2.1000
3	3.0301	3.0604	3.0909	3.1216	3.1525	3.1836	3.2149	3.2464	3.2781	3.3100
4	4.0604	4.1216	4.1836	4.2465	4.3101	4.3746	4.4399	4.5061	4.5731	4.6410
5	5.1010	5.2040	5.3091	5.4163	5.5256	5.6371	5.7507	5.8666	5.9847	6.1051
6	6.1520	6.3081	6.4684	6.6330	6.8019	6.9753	7.1533	7.3359	7.5233	7.7156
7	7.2135	7.4343	7.6625	7.8983	8.1420	8.3938	8.6540	8.9228	9.2004	9.4872
8	8.2857	8.5830	8.8923	9.2142	9.5491	9.8975	10.2598	10.6366	11.0285	11.4359
9	9.3685	9.7546	10.1591	10.5828	11.0266	11.4913	11.9780	12.4876	13.0210	13.5795
10	10.4622	10.9497	11.4639	12.0061	12.5779	13.1808	13.8164	14.4866	15.1929	15.9374
11	11.5668	12.1687	12.8078	13.4864	14.2068	14.9716	15.7836	16.6455	17.5603	18.5312
12	12.6825	13.4121	14.1920	15.0258	15.9171	16.8699	17.8885	18.9771	20.1407	21.3843
13	13.8093	14.6803	15.6178	16.6268	17.7130	18.8821	20.1406	21.4953	22.9534	24.5227
14	14.9474	15.9739	17.0863	18.2919	19.5986	21.0151	22.5505	24.2149	26.0192	27.9750
15	16.0969	17.2934	18.5989	20.0236	21.5786	23.2760	25.1290	27.1521	29.3609	31.7725
16	17.2579	18.6393	20.1569	21.8245	23.6575	25.6725	27.8881	30.3243	33.0034	35.9497
17	18.4304	20.0121	21.7616	23.6975	25.8404	28.2129	30.8402	33.7502	36.9737	40.5447
18	19.6147	21.4123	23.4144	25.6454	28.1324	30.9057	33.9990	37.4502	41.3013	45.5992
19	20.8109	22.8406	25.1169	27.6712	30.5390	33.7600	37.3790	41.4463	46.0185	51.1591
20	22.0190	24.2974	26.8704	29.7781	33.0660	36.7856	40.9955	45.7620	51.1601	57.2750
25	28.2432	32.0303	36.4593	41.6459	47.7271	54.8645	63.2490	73.1059	84.7009	98.3471
30	34.7849	40.5681	47.5754	56.0849	66.4388	79.0582	94.4608	113.2832	136.3075	164.4940
35	41.6603	49.9945	60.4621	73.6522	90.3203	111.4348	138.2369	172.3168	215.7108	271.0244
40	48.8864	60.4020	75.4013	95.0255	120.7998	154.7620	199.6351	259.0565	337.8824	442.5926
45	56.4811	71.8927	92.7199	121.0294	159.7002	212.7435	285.7493	386.5056	525.8587	718.9048
50	64.4632	84.5794	112.7969	152.6671	209.3480	290.3359	406.5289	573.7702	815.0836	1.16e+03

11%	12%	13%	14%	15%	16%	17%	18%	19%	20%	Periods
1.0000	1.0000	1.0000	1.0000	1.0000	1.0000	1.0000	1.0000	1.0000	1.0000	1
2.1100	2.1200	2.1300	2.1400	2.1500	2.1600	2.1700	2.1800	2.1900	2.2000	2
3.3421	3.3744	3.4069	3.4396	3.4725	3.5056	3.5389	3.5724	3.6061	3.6400	3
4.7097	4.7793	4.8498	4.9211	4.9934	5.0665	5.1405	5.2154	5.2913	5.3680	4
6.2278	6.3528	6.4803	6.6101	6.7424	6.8771	7.0144	7.1542	7.2966	7.4416	5
7.9129	8.1152	8.3227	8.5355	8.7537	8.9775	9.2068	9.4420	9.6830	9.9299	6
9.7833	10.0890	10.4047	10.7305	11.0668	11.4139	11.7720	12.1415	12.5227	12.9159	7
11.8594	12.2997	12.7573	13.2328	13.7268	14.2401	14.7733	15.3270	15.9020	16.4991	8
14.1640	14.7757	15.4157	16.0853	16.7858	17.5185	18.2847	19.0859	19.9234	20.7989	9
16.7220	17.5487	18.4197	19.3373	20.3037	21.3215	22.3931	23.5213	24.7089	25.9587	10
19.5614	20.6546	21.8143	23.0445	24.3493	25.7329	27.1999	28.7551	30.4035	32.1504	11
22.7132	24.1331	25.6502	27.2707	29.0017	30.8502	32.8239	34.9311	37.1802	39.5805	12
26.2116	28.0291	29.9847	32.0887	34.3519	36.7862	39.4040	42.2187	45.2445	48.4966	13
30.0949	32.3926	34.8827	37.5811	40.5047	43.6720	47.1027	50.8180	54.8409	59.1959	14
34.4054	37.2797	40.4175	43.8424	47.5804	51.6595	56.1101	60.9653	66.2607	72.0351	15
39.1899	42.7533	46.6717	50.9804	55.7175	60.9250	66.6488	72.9390	79.8502	87.4421	16
44.5008	48.8837	53.7391	59.1176	65.0751	71.6730	78.9792	87.0680	96.0218	105.9306	17
50.3959	55.7497	61.7251	68.3941	75.8364	84.1407	93.4056	103.7403	115.2659	128.1167	18
56.9395	63.4397	70.7494	78.9692	88.2118	98.6032	110.2846	123.4135	138.1664	154.7400	19
64.2028	72.0524	80.9468	91.0249	102.4436	115.3797	130.0329	146.6280	165.4180	186.6880	20
114.4133	133.3339	155.6196	181.8708	212.7930	249.2140	292.1049	342.6035	402.0425	471.9811	25
199.0209	241.3327	293.1992	356.7868	434.7451	530.3117	647.4391	790.9480	966.7122	1.18e+03	30
341.5896	431.6635	546.6808	693.5727	881.1702	1.12e+03	1.43e+03	1.82e+03	2.31e+03	2.95e+03	35
581.8261	767.0914	1.01e+03	1.34e+03	1.78e+03	2.36e+03	3.13e+03	4.16e+03	5.53e+03	7.34e+03	40
986.6386	1.36e+03	1.87e+03	2.59e+03	3.59e+03	4.97e+03	6.88e+03	9.53e+03	1.32e+04	1.83e+04	45
1.67e+03	2.40e+03	3.46e+03	4.99e+03	7.22e+03	1.04e+04	1.51e+04	2.18e+04	3.15e+04	4.55e+04	50

Present Value of $1

$$PVIF = 1/(1+k)^n$$

Periods	1%	2%	3%	4%	5%	6%	7%	8%	9%	10%
1	0.9901	0.9804	0.9709	0.9615	0.9524	0.9434	0.9346	0.9259	0.9174	0.9091
2	0.9803	0.9612	0.9426	0.9246	0.9070	0.8900	0.8734	0.8573	0.8417	0.8264
3	0.9706	0.9423	0.9151	0.8890	0.8638	0.8396	0.8163	0.7938	0.7722	0.7513
4	0.9610	0.9238	0.8885	0.8548	0.8227	0.7921	0.7629	0.7350	0.7084	0.6830
5	0.9515	0.9057	0.8626	0.8219	0.7835	0.7473	0.7130	0.6806	0.6499	0.6209
6	0.9420	0.8880	0.8375	0.7903	0.7462	0.7050	0.6663	0.6302	0.5963	0.5645
7	0.9327	0.8706	0.8131	0.7599	0.7107	0.6651	0.6227	0.5835	0.5470	0.5132
8	0.9235	0.8535	0.7894	0.7307	0.6768	0.6274	0.5820	0.5403	0.5019	0.4665
9	0.9143	0.8368	0.7664	0.7026	0.6446	0.5919	0.5439	0.5002	0.4604	0.4241
10	0.9053	0.8203	0.7441	0.6756	0.6139	0.5584	0.5083	0.4632	0.4224	0.3855
11	0.8963	0.8043	0.7224	0.6496	0.5847	0.5268	0.4751	0.4289	0.3875	0.3505
12	0.8874	0.7885	0.7014	0.6246	0.5568	0.4970	0.4440	0.3971	0.3555	0.3186
13	0.8787	0.7730	0.6810	0.6006	0.5303	0.4688	0.4150	0.3677	0.3262	0.2897
14	0.8700	0.7579	0.6611	0.5775	0.5051	0.4423	0.3878	0.3405	0.2992	0.2633
15	0.8613	0.7430	0.6419	0.5553	0.4810	0.4173	0.3624	0.3152	0.2745	0.2394
16	0.8528	0.7284	0.6232	0.5339	0.4581	0.3936	0.3387	0.2919	0.2519	0.2176
17	0.8444	0.7142	0.6050	0.5134	0.4363	0.3714	0.3166	0.2703	0.2311	0.1978
18	0.8360	0.7002	0.5874	0.4936	0.4155	0.3503	0.2959	0.2502	0.2120	0.1799
19	0.8277	0.6864	0.5703	0.4746	0.3957	0.3305	0.2765	0.2317	0.1945	0.1635
20	0.8195	0.6730	0.5537	0.4564	0.3769	0.3118	0.2584	0.2145	0.1784	0.1486
25	0.7798	0.6095	0.4776	0.3751	0.2953	0.2330	0.1842	0.1460	0.1160	0.0923
30	0.7419	0.5521	0.4120	0.3083	0.2314	0.1741	0.1314	0.0994	0.0754	0.0573
35	0.7059	0.5000	0.3554	0.2534	0.1813	0.1301	0.0937	0.0676	0.0490	0.0356
40	0.6717	0.4529	0.3066	0.2083	0.1420	0.0972	0.0668	0.0460	0.0318	0.0221
45	0.6391	0.4102	0.2644	0.1712	0.1113	0.0727	0.0476	0.0313	0.0207	0.0137
50	0.6080	0.3715	0.2281	0.1407	0.0872	0.0543	0.0339	0.0213	0.0134	0.0085

Present Value And Future Value Factors

11%	12%	13%	14%	15%	16%	17%	18%	19%	20%	Periods
0.9009	0.8929	0.8850	0.8772	0.8696	0.8621	0.8547	0.8475	0.8403	0.8333	1
0.8116	0.7972	0.7831	0.7695	0.7561	0.7432	0.7305	0.7182	0.7062	0.6944	2
0.7312	0.7118	0.6931	0.6750	0.6575	0.6407	0.6244	0.6086	0.5934	0.5787	3
0.6587	0.6355	0.6133	0.5921	0.5718	0.5523	0.5337	0.5158	0.4987	0.4823	4
0.5935	0.5674	0.5428	0.5194	0.4972	0.4761	0.4561	0.4371	0.4190	0.4019	5
0.5346	0.5066	0.4803	0.4556	0.4323	0.4104	0.3898	0.3704	0.3521	0.3349	6
0.4817	0.4523	0.4251	0.3996	0.3759	0.3538	0.3332	0.3139	0.2959	0.2791	7
0.4339	0.4039	0.3762	0.3506	0.3269	0.3050	0.2848	0.2660	0.2487	0.2326	8
0.3909	0.3606	0.3329	0.3075	0.2843	0.2630	0.2434	0.2255	0.2090	0.1938	9
0.3522	0.3220	0.2946	0.2697	0.2472	0.2267	0.2080	0.1911	0.1756	0.1615	10
0.3173	0.2875	0.2607	0.2366	0.2149	0.1954	0.1778	0.1619	0.1476	0.1346	11
0.2858	0.2567	0.2307	0.2076	0.1869	0.1685	0.1520	0.1372	0.1240	0.1122	12
0.2575	0.2292	0.2042	0.1821	0.1625	0.1452	0.1299	0.1163	0.1042	0.0935	13
0.2320	0.2046	0.1807	0.1597	0.1413	0.1252	0.1110	0.0985	0.0876	0.0779	14
0.2090	0.1827	0.1599	0.1401	0.1229	0.1079	0.0949	0.0835	0.0736	0.0649	15
0.1883	0.1631	0.1415	0.1229	0.1069	0.0930	0.0811	0.0708	0.0618	0.0541	16
0.1696	0.1456	0.1252	0.1078	0.0929	0.0802	0.0693	0.0600	0.0520	0.0451	17
0.1528	0.1300	0.1108	0.0946	0.0808	0.0691	0.0592	0.0508	0.0437	0.0376	18
0.1377	0.1161	0.0981	0.0829	0.0703	0.0596	0.0506	0.0431	0.0367	0.0313	19
0.1240	0.1037	0.0868	0.0728	0.0611	0.0514	0.0433	0.0365	0.0308	0.0261	20
0.0736	0.0588	0.0471	0.0378	0.0304	0.0245	0.0197	0.0160	0.0129	0.0105	25
0.0437	0.0334	0.0256	0.0196	0.0151	0.0116	0.0090	0.0070	0.0054	0.0042	30
0.0259	0.0189	0.0139	0.0102	0.0075	0.0055	0.0041	0.0030	0.0023	0.0017	35
0.0154	0.0107	0.0075	0.0053	0.0037	0.0026	0.0019	0.0013	0.0010	0.0007	40
0.0091	0.0061	0.0041	0.0027	0.0019	0.0013	0.0009	0.0006	0.0004	0.0003	45
0.0054	0.0035	0.0022	0.0014	0.0009	0.0006	0.0004	0.0003	0.0002	0.0001	50

Present Value of an Annuity of $1

$$PVIFA = [1-1/(1+k)^n]/k$$

Periods	1%	2%	3%	4%	5%	6%	7%	8%	9%	10%
1	0.9901	0.9804	0.9709	0.9615	0.9524	0.9434	0.9346	0.9259	0.9174	0.9091
2	1.9704	1.9416	1.9135	1.8861	1.8594	1.8334	1.8080	1.7833	1.7591	1.7355
3	2.9410	2.8839	2.8286	2.7751	2.7232	2.6730	2.6243	2.5771	2.5313	2.4869
4	3.9020	3.8077	3.7171	3.6299	3.5460	3.4651	3.3872	3.3121	3.2397	3.1699
5	4.8534	4.7135	4.5797	4.4518	4.3295	4.2124	4.1002	3.9927	3.8897	3.7908
6	5.7955	5.6014	5.4172	5.2421	5.0757	4.9173	4.7665	4.6229	4.4859	4.3553
7	6.7282	6.4720	6.2303	6.0021	5.7864	5.5824	5.3893	5.2064	5.0330	4.8684
8	7.6517	7.3255	7.0197	6.7327	6.4632	6.2098	5.9713	5.7466	5.5348	5.3349
9	8.5660	8.1622	7.7861	7.4353	7.1078	6.8017	6.5152	6.2469	5.9952	5.7590
10	9.4713	8.9826	8.5302	8.1109	7.7217	7.3601	7.0236	6.7101	6.4177	6.1446
11	10.3676	9.7868	9.2526	8.7605	8.3064	7.8869	7.4987	7.1390	6.8052	6.4951
12	11.2551	10.5753	9.9540	9.3851	8.8633	8.3838	7.9427	7.5361	7.1607	6.8137
13	12.1337	11.3484	10.6350	9.9856	9.3936	8.8527	8.3577	7.9038	7.4869	7.1034
14	13.0037	12.1062	11.2961	10.5631	9.8986	9.2950	8.7455	8.2442	7.7862	7.3667
15	13.8651	12.8493	11.9379	11.1184	10.3797	9.7122	9.1079	8.5595	8.0607	7.6061
16	14.7179	13.5777	12.5611	11.6523	10.8378	10.1059	9.4466	8.8514	8.3126	7.8237
17	15.5623	14.2919	13.1661	12.1657	11.2741	10.4773	9.7632	9.1216	8.5436	8.0216
18	16.3983	14.9920	13.7535	12.6593	11.6896	10.8276	10.0591	9.3719	8.7556	8.2014
19	17.2260	15.6785	14.3238	13.1339	12.0853	11.1581	10.3356	9.6036	8.9501	8.3649
20	18.0456	16.3514	14.8775	13.5903	12.4622	11.4699	10.5940	9.8181	9.1285	8.5136
25	22.0232	19.5235	17.4131	15.6221	14.0939	12.7834	11.6536	10.6748	9.8226	9.0770
30	25.8077	22.3965	19.6004	17.2920	15.3725	13.7648	12.4090	11.2578	10.2737	9.4269
35	29.4086	24.9986	21.4872	18.6646	16.3742	14.4982	12.9477	11.6546	10.5668	9.6442
40	32.8347	27.3555	23.1148	19.7928	17.1591	15.0463	13.3317	11.9246	10.7574	9.7791
45	36.0945	29.4902	24.5187	20.7200	17.7741	15.4558	13.6055	12.1084	10.8812	9.8628
50	39.1961	31.4236	25.7298	21.4822	18.2559	15.7619	13.8007	12.2335	10.9617	9.9148

11%	12%	13%	14%	15%	16%	17%	18%	19%	20%	Periods
0.9009	0.8929	0.8850	0.8772	0.8696	0.8621	0.8547	0.8475	0.8403	0.8333	1
1.7125	1.6901	1.6681	1.6467	1.6257	1.6052	1.5852	1.5656	1.5465	1.5278	2
2.4437	2.4018	2.3612	2.3216	2.2832	2.2459	2.2096	2.1743	2.1399	2.1065	3
3.1024	3.0373	2.9745	2.9137	2.8550	2.7982	2.7432	2.6901	2.6386	2.5887	4
3.6959	3.6048	3.5172	3.4331	3.3522	3.2743	3.1993	3.1272	3.0576	2.9906	5
4.2305	4.1114	3.9975	3.8887	3.7845	3.6847	3.5892	3.4976	3.4098	3.3255	6
4.7122	4.5638	4.4226	4.2883	4.1604	4.0386	3.9224	3.8115	3.7057	3.6046	7
5.1461	4.9676	4.7988	4.6389	4.4873	4.3436	4.2072	4.0776	3.9544	3.8372	8
5.5370	5.3282	5.1317	4.9464	4.7716	4.6065	4.4506	4.3030	4.1633	4.0310	9
5.8892	5.6502	5.4262	5.2161	5.0188	4.8332	4.6586	4.4941	4.3389	4.1925	10
6.2065	5.9377	5.6869	5.4527	5.2337	5.0286	4.8364	4.6560	4.4865	4.3271	11
6.4924	6.1944	5.9176	5.6603	5.4206	5.1971	4.9884	4.7932	4.6105	4.4392	12
6.7499	6.4235	6.1218	5.8424	5.5831	5.3423	5.1183	4.9095	4.7147	4.5327	13
6.9819	6.6282	6.3025	6.0021	5.7245	5.4675	5.2293	5.0081	4.8023	4.6106	14
7.1909	6.8109	6.4624	6.1422	5.8474	5.5755	5.3242	5.0916	4.8759	4.6755	15
7.3792	6.9740	6.6039	6.2651	5.9542	5.6685	5.4053	5.1624	4.9377	4.7296	16
7.5488	7.1196	6.7291	6.3729	6.0472	5.7487	5.4746	5.2223	4.9897	4.7746	17
7.7016	7.2497	6.8399	6.4674	6.1280	5.8178	5.5339	5.2732	5.0333	4.8122	18
7.8393	7.3658	6.9380	6.5504	6.1982	5.8775	5.5845	5.3162	5.0700	4.8435	19
7.9633	7.4694	7.0248	6.6231	6.2593	5.9288	5.6278	5.3527	5.1009	4.8696	20
8.4217	7.8431	7.3300	6.8729	6.4641	6.0971	5.7662	5.4669	5.1951	4.9476	25
8.6938	8.0552	7.4957	7.0027	6.5660	6.1772	5.8294	5.5168	5.2347	4.9789	30
8.8552	8.1755	7.5856	7.0700	6.6166	6.2153	5.8582	5.5386	5.2512	4.9915	35
8.9511	8.2438	7.6344	7.1050	6.6418	6.2335	5.8713	5.5482	5.2582	4.9966	40
9.0079	8.2825	7.6609	7.1232	6.6543	6.2421	5.8773	5.5523	5.2611	4.9986	45
9.0417	8.3045	7.6752	7.1327	6.6605	6.2463	5.8801	5.5541	5.2623	4.9995	50

INDEX

CAPITAL BUDGETING SOFTWARE SYSTEM
(INTERACTIVE VERSION)

System Installation

System Operation:
Manual Mode; Interactive Mode

Project Identification

Data Required

Initial Investment

Sale of Existing Property

Net Working Capital Changes

Positive Annual Cash Flows

Negative Annual Cash Flows

Depreciation and Salvage Value Schedule:
Manual Mode; Interactive Mode

Forgone Depreciation and Salvage Value Schedule

Cash Flow Summary

Cash Flow Analysis

Projects with Unequal Lives

Introduction

Capital Budgeting Software System is an Excel 7.0-based system that provides a framework in which to analyze capital asset investment decisions for project with an anticipated useful life of up to 40 years. The system is organized in a workbook format. Individual worksheets address the individual components of the capital budgeting decision.

Name of worksheet	Time period(s)
Project Identification	n/a
Initial Investment	zero
Sale of Existing Asset	zero
Net Working Capital Changes	zero
Positive Annual Cash Flows	1 through n
Negative Annual Cash Flows	1 through n
Depreciation and Salvage Value Schedule	1 through n
Forgone Depreciation and Salvage Value Schedule	1 through n
Cash Flow Summary	0 through n
Cash Flow Analysis	0 through n
Projects with Unequal Lives	0 through n

Each worksheet requires input from the user as indicated by a cell address in parentheses. For example, *Purchase price (F7)* means that the user should place the purchase price in cell F7.

Other line items are accompanied by the phrase (*do not input*). In these cases, the system is programmed to produce the result. No user input is required.

System Installation

To install *Capital Budgeting Software System*, save C_Budget.xls on a hard drive with at least 500kb of available disk space.

The *Capital Budgeting Software System* should be placed on the user's hard drive, so that if any of the code is erased inadvertently, the diskette version of the program can be used to reinstall the system.

System Operation

On the Windows task bar, click the "Start" button, then choose "run." In the dialogue box, type the full path name of the file, for example,

c:\c_budget\c_budget.xls

where c:\c_budget is the path of the file. The first worksheet will appear – "Project."

Manual Mode

To use the system as a conventional spreadsheet, input the information requested in cells F6, F7, F10, F11, and F13 of "Project." Proceed to the next sheet, by clicking the tab at the bottom of the spreadsheet – "Initial_Investment." Input the requested information. Continue this process through the following sheets:

- Sale_of_Existing
- Working_Capital_Changes
- Positive_CFs
- Negative_CFs
- Depreciation
- Forgone_Depreciation
- CF_Summary
- Unequal Lives (as applicable).

Interactive Mode

Click the "Main Menu" button on "Project" worksheet.

- To analyze cash flows for a project and compute internal rate of return, net present value, and profitability index, select "Capital Budgeting:"
  - enter project name and duration of project in years, then click "Next;"
  - enter name of person or group performing the analysis, applicable income tax rate, and capital gains tax rate;
  - click "Next" and continue the input as requested;
  - the "Exit" button will terminate the Interactive Mode and place the cursor in the last field of input.
- To analyze mutually exclusive projects with unequal lives, select "Unequal Lives" on the Main Menu and press "Next."
- To return to the Manual Mode, select "Manual Mode" and press "Next."

  The following sections describe the specific data required in each case.

Project Identification

Data Required

- The individual or group responsible for the project analysis.
- Income tax rate – marginal corporate tax rate.
- Capital gains tax rate – tax rate that applies to gains or losses on sale of capital assets. In some cases, the capital gains tax rate will be identical to the marginal corporate tax rate. However, in every case, both rates must be input even if they are identical.

Initial Investment

A project may either be purchased, constructed, or transferred in from another division of the firm, or some combination of these. Each such cost should be recorded. In the case of transferred equipment or property, the opportunity cost is relevant, that is, the next best alternative use of the property. If installation costs are required, these should also be recorded in the appropriate cell (manual mode) or text box (interactive mode).

USER'S MANUAL

Sale of Existing Property

When existing property must be considered, the decision is referred to as a *replacement decision*. The required data is:

- anticipated gross proceeds of the sale
- the current book value of the existing property
- the system automatically computes the capital gain or loss and the tax impact of the capital gain or loss.

Net Working Capital Changes

When a new project is adopted, changes in the level of current assets and current liabilities often occur. The user should include these changes in the appropriate line or text box under the appropriate categories – *working capital increases* or *working capital decreases*. The working capital line items are:

- inventory
- accounts receivable
- other asset categories
- payables and accruals
- deferred taxes.

Positive Annual Cash Flows

Positive annual cash flows occur beginning in year 1 of the subsequent years. Either increases in future cash inflows or decreases in future cash outflows qualify as positive cash flows. Increased revenues and reduced or eliminated expenses should be recorded by the user net of income tax and adjusted for inflation, as appropriate.

Also decreases in net working capital have a positive impact on cash flow:

- inventory decreases
- accounts receivable decreases
- other asset category decreases
- payables and accruals increases
- deferred tax increases.

In addition, it is assumed that any net working capital increases (negative cash flow) recognized in the year of acquisition (time zero) will be reversed (positive cash flow) at the end of the project's useful life (time *n*). Accordingly, in manual mode, the user should place this reversal at the appropriate point on the time line in the worksheet. In interactive mode, the amount of the reversal is requested in the last text box of year 1.

Neither (1) changes in working capital during the life of the project nor (2) reversals of time zero working capital should be adjusted for income taxes.

Up to 40 years of cash flows may be input by the user. Totals, that is, net positive cash flows, are automatically computed by the system.

Negative Annual Cash Flows

Negative annual cash flows occur beginning in year 1 of the subsequent years. Either increases in future expenses or decreases in future revenues qualify as negative cash flows. Increased expenses and reduced or eliminated revenues should be recorded by the user net of income tax and adjusted for inflation as appropriate.

Also increases in net working capital have a negative impact on cash flow:

- inventory increases
- accounts receivable increases
- other asset category increases
- payables and accruals decreases
- deferred tax decreases.

In addition, it is assumed that any net working capital decreases (positive cash flow) recognized in the year of acquisition (time zero) will be reversed (negative cash flow) at the end of the project's useful life (time *n*). Accordingly, in manual mode, the user should place this reversal at the appropriate point on the time line in the worksheet. In interactive mode, the amount of the reversal is requested in the last text box of year 1.

Neither (1) changes in working capital during the life of the project nor (2) reversals of time zero working capital should be adjusted for income taxes.

USER'S MANUAL

Up to 40 years of cash flows may be input by the user. Totals, that is, net negative cash flows, are automatically computed by the system.

Depreciation and Salvage Value Schedule

The initial investment of a capital project consists of depreciable assets (excluding land which may not be depreciated). This schedule allows the investment to be recorded in the appropriate depreciation method line. The user has the choice of several depreciation methods:

Manual Mode

In manual mode, asset depreciation is based on input as follows.

- Straight line with no salvage value. Amount and years of useful life must be input.
- Straight line with salvage value. Amount, years of useful life, and antici-pated salvage must be input. The salvage value is input in cell F20 and in the appropriate year on the time line.
- 200% declining balance – 3-year, 5-year, 7-year, and 10-year.
- 150% declining balance – 5-year, 7-year, 10-year, 12-year, 15-year, and 20-year.

In each case, the amount to be depreciated is recorded in column G – rows 14–34.

In addition, for accelerated methods of depreciation (which depreciate to a zero book), any anticipated salvage value will be taxable. Accordingly, this amount should be input in the last year of actual useful life, regardless of the accelerated depreciation method selected.

Below row 40, the system automatically computes the amount of annual depreciation and the depreciation shield:

*Annual depreciation * tax rate*

Also, the salvage values are evaluated on an after-tax basis, as appropriate. The user inputs no data below row 40.

Interactive Mode

The interactive mode requires similar input as follows.

- For straight depreciation, input the amount, years of useful life, and anticipated salvage value. Enter zero if no salvage value is anticipated.
- For 200% declining balance, place the amount in the text box and select the appropriate number of years in the drop-down box.
- For 150% declining balance, place the amount in the text box and select the appropriate number of years in the drop-down box.

When appropriate depreciation has been recorded, click "OK." If additional assets are to be depreciated using another depreciation method, select "Yes" when asked "Do you wish to make additional depreciation entries?"

If a salvage value is anticipated, select "Salvage Value-Accelerated," input amount, and click "OK."

Forgone Depreciation and Salvage Value Schedule

For replacement decisions, this schedule recognizes the depreciation tax shield and salvage value that would have been realized if existing property were retained. Any sale of the existing property at time zero necessarily results in the forfeiture of future depreciation and future sale. The required information for this schedule is as follows.

- Depreciation for each year of useful life that would be possible if the existing property were retained.
- Forgone salvage value in the appropriate year if the existing property were not disposed of at time zero.
- Projected book value of the existing property at the time of the forgone sale.

The system automatically computes the forgone depreciation tax shield and the forgone salvage value, net of tax.

Cash Flow Summary

The user is required to input the cost of capital in cell F35.

The system automatically accumulates all cash flows from the preceding worksheets. In addition, the present value of each of the net cash flows is computed automatically.

Cash Flow Analysis

Based on results in the Cash Flow Summary, this worksheet automatically computes:

- internal rate of return (IRR)
- net present value (NPV)
- profitability index (PI).

A project is acceptable if:

- IRR equals or exceeds the cost of capital;
- NPV equals or exceeds 0;
- PI equals or exceeds 1.

Projects with Unequal Lives

For mutually exclusive projects with different useful lives, this worksheet permits the analysis of their effective annual cash flows for each year of useful life. A total of five projects may be compared. In each case, NPV, years of project life, and the cost of capital must be input. The *equivalent annual annuity* is the effective annual cash flow. The project with the highest EAA is the optimal project.